MARRYING
GEORGE CLOONEY

PRAISE FOR
MARRYING GEORGE CLOONEY

"This book, this perfect gem, makes me want to stay in a
midlife crisis forever. It's that good! Funny. Delicious. Poignant.
Someday I hope to describe a relationship like that—but in the
meantime, this book is staying next to me on the night table."
—CARLA SINGER, TELEVISION AND MOVIE PRODUCER

"Amy Ferris is the menopausal David Sedaris."
—SEAN STRUB, EDITOR AND FOUNDER OF *POZ MAGAZINE*

"I knew that Amy Ferris was a brilliant satirist,
but in this marvel of a book she guides us into deeper and
deeper considerations of everything that matters: mothers,
partners, friendships, work—and the body's many betrayals.
I laughed, but was also moved to tears. Every line was
a revelation—read it and your thoughts about your
own life will be forever changed."
—CAROL JENKINS, PRESIDENT, THE WOMEN'S MEDIA CENTER

"Prepare to laugh, cry, and not be able to put *Marrying George Clooney* down till you've read every delicious page. Breathes there a woman of a certain age who can't relate, especially at 3:00 am."
—GLORIA FELDT, CO-AUTHOR WITH KATHLEEN TURNER OF THE BEST-SELLER, *SEND YOURSELF ROSES;* BLOGGER AT GLORIAFELDT.COM

"I absolutely love this book! Amy tells it like it is, she opens her heart and shares her feelings with no hidden agenda. It is very refreshing. She made me really laugh, and she made me reflect on my own experiences with menopause. I could not put the book down, and I did not want the book to end."
—DR. SILVIA JIMENEZ KRAUSE, SURGEON, COLUMNIST, WOMEN'S HEALTH ADVOCATE

"Amy Ferris is the most original voice of memory to come along in the last decade."
—CAROLYN HOWARD-JOHNSON, MULTI AWARD-WINNING NOVELIST AND POET

"*Marrying George Clooney* takes you for a ride into the wacky, wonderful, marvelously moving mind of a modern menopausal woman. It's a no holes barred exploration of what makes ALL of us tick . . . men and women! I applaud Ferris's tenacity, humor, and courage. Raging hormones will never be the same!"
—KRISTI ZEA, DIRECTOR, *EVERYBODY KNOWS ELIZABETH MURRAY*; PRODUCTION DESIGNER, *REVOLUTIONARY ROAD, THE DEPARTED, GOODFELLAS,* AND *SILENCE OF THE LAMBS*

"The profundity sneaks up on you in Amy Ferris's irresistible little memoir. One second you're laughing your ass off, because Amy is bitching about her husband's Cialis-fueled sex drive, and the next you're crying because she's curled up on a hospital bed with her dying mother. Ultimately, *Marrying George Clooney* is so surprisingly radical, because it's so frickin' real. You can't help but see yourself in Amy's wanderings and wonderings, and even forgive yourself a little in the process."
—COURTNEY E. MARTIN, AUTHOR OF *PERFECT GIRLS, STARVING DAUGHTERS*

"Reading Amy Ferris is about laughing out loud, essential reading for peri to post menopausal women and for those who love them. Amy makes you want to tag her online to share your Mommy & Me dementia stories."
—JULIE DASH, FILM DIRECTOR *DAUGHTERS OF THE DUST, FUNNY VALENTINES,* AND *THE ROSA PARKS STORY*

MARRYING
GEORGE CLOONEY

*Confessions from
a Midlife Crisis*

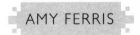

AMY FERRIS

SEAL PRESS

Marrying George Clooney
Confessions from a Midlife Crisis

Published by Seal Press
A Member of the Perseus Books Group
1700 Fourth Street
Berkeley, CA 94710

Library of Congress Cataloging-in-Publication Data
Ferris, Amy Schor.
 Marrying George Clooney : confessions from a midlife crisis /
Amy Ferris.
    p. cm.
 ISBN 978-1-58005-297-9
1. Menopause—Humor. I. Title.
 PN6231.M453F47 2009
 814'.6—dc22

                                    2009010282

9 8 7 6 5 4 3 2

Cover and Interior design by Domini Dragoone
Printed in the United States of America by Maple-Vail
Distributed by Publishers Group West

"All you need is a dollar and a dream."

–New York State Lottery Slogan

*(And I would add one and/or two, or three,
great women who believe in you.)*

This book is dedicated to:
JANE DYSTEL
MIRIAM GODERICH
and
KRISTA LYONS

PREFACE

These are my musings.
My journey.
My personal feelings and my
* experiences.*
The view from my window.

MY LIFE.

My husband has graciously allowed me to share the view—
our view. Some friends have graciously asked that I not name
them specifically, so I don't. Others were fine and loved being
named, and quite a few names have been changed. But in most
incidences, names are not mentioned.

And in life, there are often many, many different points of view. I mean, really—how many folks look at the exact same painting or hear a piece of music and see or hear something completely different?

I encourage any and all to find a view, from their window, and to please write it all down, share your story, speak your truth.

These are my musings from (almost exclusively) the middle of the night.

C*O*NTENTS

MIDLIFE

I think it's safe to say that it usually starts somewhere around forty, forty-five. I AM FIFTY-FOUR. I doubt highly that I will live to a hundred and eight. You never know, though. Someone, somewhere can come up with a miracle pill or some sort of reverse-aging serum. But for right now, I'm hopeful I'll reach eighty-five. Barring my being struck by a bus at a crosswalk, or shot down by a demented stranger as I stand in line at any post office or a peace rally.

I am hopeful.

For some women midlife equals the empty nest; their children have all grown or are growing up, no longer needing them. Some are finding themselves single after years of marriage or partnerships, divorce, death . . . and/ or unexpected separations. Some, like me, are childless and experiencing the pain of watching a parent disappear right before their eyes from dementia or Alzheimer's. My friend Amy calls this "Mama-pause." And for some, it's the trifecta—the kids are grown, the partners are gone, and the parents are slipping away.

So here's to us: the BOLD, AUDACIOUS, STRONG, GORGEOUS, TALENTED, AND POWERFUL WOMEN who are proving that fifty is fabulous and midlife is no longer a final destination but an express subway stop. We are not just reinventing ourselves—we are in fact reinventing the entire fucking wheel . . . and some, like me, doing it in the middle of the night.

MEN. OH. PAUSE. REWIND.

Imagine this scenario if you will: You're in the Holland or Lincoln Tunnel—all of a sudden, without a warning, all the lights go out, including all the headlights on all the cars. YOU'RE STUCK. There's no going forward; there's no going backward. Complete and utter darkness. And you know in your soul that others are going through the exact same thing—but no one, not one person, gets out of their car. Doors are locked. Windows are rolled up. Seat belts are tightened. Everyone just sits, looking straight ahead, waiting, waiting, waiting. For. A. Light. To. Flicker. At. The. End. Of. The. Tunnel.

WELCOME TO MENOPAUSE.
Exit 36B on the highway called Life.

Perhaps this is a good time for me to rattle off some of the symptoms of my personal menopausal journey. This journey, by the way, began with one step. While I don't consider myself "an exercise type o' gal," I have been spinning almost nonstop for the past few years. I have been *depressed, anxious, forgetful, lost in a fog, angry, and resentful, with an emphasis on angry. I have been filled with tremendous hope and, in the next unexpected moment, filled with the exact amount of despair. I have cried uncontrollably from my gut, and I have laughed from the depths of my soul.* I have felt like throwing my life away, as in literally jumping off a bridge. I have witnessed my body grow one full size while sleeping soundly; I have been able to pull and form my new love handles into the same animal-like shapes that I was once able to create out of balloons. I could continue, but I think you get the idea.

IN THE MIDST OF THIS FRESH HELL,
I DECIDED TO QUIT SMOKING. I'm not sure if it was an act of courage or just simply self-destructive behavior. After thirty-two years of smoking, I wanted to stop filling my lungs with tar and nicotine, even though, simultaneously, I was looking for that perfect bridge. For whatever reason, the "clean panty theory" played over in my mind. I could actually hear my mother (and I believe all mothers) saying, "Don't forget to wear clean panties in case you get into an accident. You may need to be rushed to the hospital." I simply substituted "clean panties" with "clean lungs." Dare anyone find me with dirty lungs after I took the plunge off a bridge.

So, I quit smoking. Much to my husband's grand delight, not to mention that of my friends and family, I decided to divorce the one constant that kept me from experiencing my feelings fully. Every time I would feel anxious, sad, depressed, nervous, bitter, resentful, fearful, and hopeless, I would light up—and almost instantaneously, those feelings would dissolve. Well, actually, in truth they didn't dissolve—they were simply pushed down to the subterranean level of suppression where they had lived and thrived for my entire adult life. Oh, were they in for a treat! They were about to experience sunlight for the first time.

So, not only were my hormones doing a ferocious dance, now my suppressed, discarded feelings were vying for attention.

THIS IS THE POINT IN THE STORY WHERE I GET TO INTRODUCE MY HUSBAND. Please raise your hand if any of you have turned into the devil doll on a dime. You know what I'm talking about—that moment when your husband (or wife or partner) says or does something trivial, innocuous, a casual throwaway, and without a moment's hesitation you respond by burning a hole in their heart with your tongue. And it's all downhill from there. The only word that comes to mind to describe my behavior is vile. The only word to describe my husband's reaction is stunned, although I have a feeling that a psychiatrist (not even necessarily a good one) would say that Ken was scared to death of my irrational and unpredictable behavior and staying as far away from me as humanly possible.

Along with herbs—black cohosh, peony, passionflower, and a dab of progesterone cream twice a day, I decided to go back to weekly acupuncture treatments. Kathleen, my acupuncturist, said, and I'm quoting, "I feel a deep seismic shift occurring inside of you, Amy."

Uh huh. So in other words, a 10.5 right on the fault line.

Most everyone who knows me knows I am a Buddhist, a practicing Buddhist for over thirty-five years. One of the exquisite tenets of Buddhism is embracing and honoring the "whole" of our lives. Not just bits and pieces, not just "the good" or "the nice" but every inch—head to toe. Buddhism also encourages and teaches that one can find—through inner resolve—the enlightened side to anything.

FYI: My mother is not a Buddhist.

Along with weight gain and mental anguish, insomnia

is yet another "side dish" accompanying menopause.
So, late one night while unable to sleep and tossing a coin—heads, Ambien; tails, Ambien—it occurred to me that it was time for me to put into practice what I deeply believe: to (A) TRULY EMBRACE AND LOVE EVERY SINGLE PART OF ME—not just the good and kind and generous but the bad and unattractive and mentally unstable, and to (B) FIND THE ENLIGHTENED SIDE. My mother couldn't deal with my feelings, wanting me to ignore them, suppress them, hide them, but it was my obligation and responsibility to acknowledge and hold dear the privilege of my very own life.

Every single woman I know, without exception, has experienced or will experience some deep inner turmoil or upheaval because of menopause. It is a part of being a woman. Period. I have known women of great equilibrium to wobble horrifically because they were in the process of dealing with this huge change of life. The good news: Most women credit this hell as the single most profound experience that has enabled them to uncover their own greatness. I can definitely embrace that.

And here's the enlightened side: Menopause is just like couture fashion. Some of it is just really ugly.

WELCOME TO MY WORLD. . . .

ONE

GOOGLE
& AMBIEN

Okay, so I started with one half of a 5mg and have worked
myself up to two full 5mg. Which now equals 10mg, and
I still refuse to ask my doctor for a prescription for 10mg,
because I don't want him to think that I'm not completely
attached to the notion that I can't even fall asleep without
taking this TINY LITTLE FUCKING PINK PILL, which by
the way would be white if I were taking a 10mg. Nothing
is helping. NOTHING. I wake up. I STARE. I think. I THINK
SOME MORE. I go for another half of a 5mg. I've become an
addicted menopausal woman. My greatest fear is manifesting.
Let me tell you what an addicted menopausal woman looks
like at 3:00 AM: SHE LOOKS LIKE ROSEMARY'S BABY FROM
INSIDE THE WOMB. I roll over; my husband sleeps soundly,
snoring. Sound asleep, snoring. Although he tells me that

morning—that morning at a reasonable hour, like, say, 9:00 AM, he tells me that he, too, was up at 3:00 AM, and guess what . . . that is not true. He has not woken up in my house, because I would see him up at 3:00 AM, if in fact he really were up, which by the way he isn't, because I am up. He likes competing with me about stuff like this. Honey, I have such a headache. *No, no, I have a brain tumor.* Honey, baby, I have diarrhea. *No, no, no, I have colon cancer.* Some couples compete at skiing. Not us. We compete with bodily fluids. He is not up at 3:00 AM. I don't care what he says, or who he tells. He is not a menopausal woman. I am. I WIN. I am staring at the ceiling, asking myself the most vital of questions: "Hmmm. Another tiny, itsy-bitsy piece of Ambien?"

Let me tell you what menopausal women do at 3:00 AM: WE GOOGLE OLD BOYFRIENDS.

I don't give a shit if you're a feminist lesbian living in Vermont on a commune for retired female welders, you will google an old boyfriend at 3:00 AM, and you will sit at your computer wondering what life would be like if in fact you had married, and then divorced, that boyfriend. And if that doesn't quite satisfy your emotional thirst, you begin googling exotic locations, like, say, Belize, Tulum, Scranton . . . and then imagine going to that exotic place with your now husband but running into your old boyfriend, who is with his shiny, brand-new, hot-off-the-conveyor-belt, 2008-model wife, who is in fact young enough to be your illegitimate child if in fact you didn't have that abortion in 1985. And you look at her and think, "God, she has my eyes."

This is what I do at 3:00 AM.

Claire emails me and says I should replace "retired female welders" with "nuns." Claire has a thing about nuns. I don't know what kind of thing. I have a notion that it's spiritually related, although, with Claire, it could be a vendetta. Claire is such a cool, cool sexy woman. She hasn't a clue how deeply sensuous and stunning and funny—laugh out loud, brilliant, gorgeous, funny—she is. I know it. HOW COME WHEN OTHER PEOPLE TELL YOU HOW BRILLIANT YOU ARE, YOU JUST STARE BLANKLY AND SAY, "REALLY?" Is it that we don't really believe that people feel that way, and we just want to press them until they bleed, or is it that we don't believe anyone can feel that way about us, especially when we're sweating profusely from every pore because a hot flash has decided to enter our vaginal highway and has pushed itself up and out of us. Every single inch can now experience hydration. Perhaps this was something you weren't thinking would happen in the middle of a dreamy, sexy ultraromantic kind of evening. A six-course meal with champagne flowing endlessly—all in a cozy corner booth at Ouest restaurant, sitting next to the man (or woman) of your dreams—in my case, my husband. *Well, baby, think again.* MENOPAUSE DOES NOT DISCRIMINATE. *I like to think of my midlife crisis as the ultimate punishment for never really wanting to have children.* There were moments, actual hours, that I wanted desperately to have kids—but just as much as I wanted to have children for those few minutes per year, in a rapid moment, that desire would vanish and be replaced by Barneys biannual warehouse-clothing-everything-70-percent-off sale. That's the god's (small g—I'm a Buddhist) honest truth. Children vs. Barneys. And this is the payback. You sweat, you scratch, you itch, and you want to rip your hair out in clumps. "No, no, I'm fine, thank you; I'm just so yes, sad, so sad that I . . . missed . . . the . . . me . . . and the, the . . . the Me & Ro jewelry sale. I can't even think straight."

This is what happens to menopausal women. We lie about everything. We cover our asses, which, by the way, mysteriously grow at night. But here's the good news: I can be a Macy's Day parade float—the other Disney character that stopped getting her period and all her fucking mouse friends abandoned her. You know, the suicidal one, Sylvia Mouse.

My husband wants to know why I google old boyfriends.

"It's 3 o'clock in the morning. You're asleep. Most of those guys, by the way, are . . . dead." (This is where he looks at me in a strange, almost peculiar way, as if to say, "Dead? Oh really?" So I continue. . . .) "Some have become born-again Christian evangelists. *(Completely true.)* David, or as he's now called, Father Brother David, is someone I grew up with, shared (many) a joint with, bought Quaaludes with—is now an Evangelist; he has his own church. He was, by the way, stoned out of his mind every single day. Then he apparently found god, like most folks who are about to be hauled off to prison—they fall to their knees and shout up to the heavens, 'Jesus, take me! I can see you. I am your child. I will spread your word and make you a ton of money and I will buy a big, big, big church and renovate it with lots of gold inlay and paint it primary colors and I will never, ever—swear to Jesus

Christ my Lord and savior—I swear that I will never, ever smoke weed again.' And for the record, I never dated David. We were friends. I might've slept with him. But sleeping with someone was—is—definitely not the same as a boyfriend. And when you run out of old boyfriends, you google old friends, old neighbors—and sometimes when you're trying to be really creative, you google alphabetically. And sometimes a big huge surprise pops up . . . one guy . . . turns out became a pretty famous rock 'n' roll musician and is living in Northern California, and apparently—get this—is now completely, totally deaf. I would've never known that if I hadn't googled him at 3:00 AM."

That's what I tell my husband, who at this point wonders out loud who he should google. I point to the computer: "I DARE YOU—GO AHEAD, GOOGLE HER." The minute I make that veiled threat, he gets bored.

Which makes me think, *who the fuck googles me?* Which old dead, deaf boyfriend? I shudder at the thought. And do they know that I'm married—do they know my married name? And the biggest cosmic question: Is the same person that I'm googling, googling me at the same moment—are we googling simultaneously?

D&AD FATH&R

*Something else I do in the
middle of the night.*

I talk to my father.

My father does not answer me.

It's a very one-sided conversation.

*Mostly I say/ask, "For god's sake,
Dad, why'd you die?"*

SPAS

Day spas.

Weekend retreats.

Exotic getaways.

Costa Rica.

St. Moritz.

Vermont.

Maine.

Vienna, Venice, Rome, Verona.

Jamaica (man), and Australia.

And what's almost off-the-charts groovy, when you decide to inquire (online) about a Relais & Chateaux five-star luxury hotel-slash-spa in the South of France: Sometimes, but not always, sometimes the concierge responds instantly. It's like

IM-ing, except you don't expect Madame or Mademoiselle Francine when she responds with the "all-inclusive" five-day/ seven-spa treatments per day/per person including high tea and coffee enemas. The all-inclusive price—listing all the amenities—seems equivalent to a yearly salary. I often respond with: "Oh, no, not Hotel—I was trying to find the Hostel Villa Gallici. You know, shared showers."

Then I feel humiliated and embarrassed. I don't google retreats for a few days. Fearing that the word is out on me. A big red slash going through my name: Impostor. I am a spa retreat/ luxury hotel stalker. I make phony reservations, not unlike when I was a child and called the neighbors asking if their refrigerator was running, and then when they said yes, I howled with laughter and then suddenly screamed, "Well, you better go and catch it!" Much to my horror, I was banished to a week of reading. Phone privileges were taken from me. As I look back at this, what strikes me is not that I made phony phone calls but that I actually thought "Well, you better go and catch it!" was funny.

Makes me wonder if there is such a thing as a "Google warning" or the "Google police."

I ASK MY HUSBAND IF WE CAN CHANGE OUR NAMES AND MOVE TO CANADA.

He says no.

FOUR

SHOE DATING

I think a lot about "shoe dating" between the hours of 3:00 AM and 5:00 PM.

Shoes, one of my all-time very favorite topics, as well as shopping pleasures. That's called a twofer. I love shoes. I've loved shoes my whole life. And in truth, for the first six years of my life I thought my father's name was Buster Brown. Can you imagine how devastated I was when I found out his name was Sam?

My very favorite part of going back to school was back-to-school shoes. Actually, it was my only favorite part of going back to school. While I wasn't too fond of having to break in my new shoes, it seemed like an awfully small price to pay to own a new pair of ox-blood, round-toed Weejun loafers. Even now, when I close my eyes and inhale, I can still smell that leather. But this is not about back-to-school shoes, or new Weejuns, so let me get right to the point.

It's about shoe dating. I have often wondered if shoes could pick out a partner. . . .

For example, do you really think a pair of black Florsheim lace-ups, say men's size 11, would ever have the courage, the all-out ballsy courage, to ask out a pair of women's size 9 backless Manolo Blahniks on a date? Hello, Earth to Florsheim, come in, Florsheim—that would go under the category of *"fantasy."* However, I'm pretty sure that coupling a men's size 10 Merrell with a women's size 9 Bass or any style of Nike would last about two, two and a half years.

A pair of yellow patent with black stitching J.P.Tod's driving shoes, on the other hand, would never, ever, ever look twice at a pair of Tevas, either in leather or fabric, especially with a pair of socks—although I can imagine, with enough alcohol, a one-night stand, and I can also imagine some kind of weird stalking thing happening. That would go under the category of *"restraining order."*

And Marc Jacobs would never, not in this lifetime, be caught dead on the same side of the street with any pair of Crocs, regardless of whether one or both feet were planted firmly on the pedals of a Harley Sportster 883. That goes under the category of *"assisted suicide."* And a pair of three-and-a-half-inch black patent pointy Christian Louboutins can catch the eye of a pair of Prada suede chukka boots in about three seconds flat.

Sometimes it's just about plain unadulterated passion—the kind of pairing that often happens in loft-type elevators and/or smoky jazz clubs. No first names or phone numbers are exchanged, but god's name is invoked more often in a short period of time than in an entire lifetime of churchgoing. The heels on those shoes are frequently replaced and repaired due to excessive European travel. They are also envied and talked about behind their sling backs. Ever wondered if a pair of Kenneth Cole married a pair of Cole Haans what that hyphenation would look like? It would look like Kenneth Cole-Haan. And that would go under the category of *"power couple."*

And if Timberland boots dated Rockport shoes, my guess is they would vacation in Maine, probably in Kennebunkport, and somewhere down the road, say in about eight years, there would be a sexual scandal. That would go under the category of *"Presidential hopeful."*

And let's not forget Thom McAn, because chances are everyone else will.

Let me tell you about a pairing I saw in my very own closet: *a pair of sexy, sequined, kitten-heeled thongs looking very much like YSL,*

standing right next to a pair of good, solid, comfy, sexy,

worn-in Frye boots. Two very opposite, strong-willed, smart

shoes. Standing toe-to-toe.

AND THAT WOULD GO UNDER THE CATEGORY OF
"EQUAL FOOTING."

FIVE

WRITING A NOVELLA

Sometimes, when I really can't sleep, when nothing, ABSOLUTELY NOTHING, works at all, I'll ruminate (seriously) about writing a novella at 3:00 AM.

I bound out of bed, go to my computer, which is in my room, and sit proudly at my desk.

Waiting for a burst of brilliance.

Waiting.

Waiting.

Then . . .

A thought. "Maybe I should start writing another novel." Fuck novella. A novel seems big and bountiful and "Pulitzer"

worthy—a novella seems . . . oh, I don't know . . . tiny.
Okay, maybe not tiny—tiny is not the right word. Thin
perhaps? No, no . . . not thin. "Oh, it was such a . . . thin
book." Sounds like a health issue, a little too bulimic. I can
see myself right now sitting in front of the Novella Tribunal:
Steve Martin, Philip Roth, David Sedaris, Anna Quindlen,
and Calvin Trillin.

DAVID: Tiny?

AMY: Well, not tiny as in small, tiny as in . . .

DAVID: Trinket?

STEVE: Excusssssse me . . . *Shopgirl* was a huge, huge
bestseller.

PHILIP: Adored the movie, despised the book.

(All eyes on Philip. A meaningful pause, then . . .)

DAVID: Heterosexual love sells.

PHILIP: Heterosexual infidelity sells.

CALVIN: *Love sells. Period. Love sells in every language.*

DAVID: Homosexual love does much better in paperback.

PHILIP: Hmmmm.

CALVIN: Hmmmm.

ANNA: Buy foreign.

DAVID: Foreign rights?

ANNA (extremely agitated): Come on, guys. Wake the fuck up. The U.S. money market is crumbling, right before our eyes, going into the toilet. Place every single penny you have in foreign banks. You'll thank me.

DAVID: Hmmmm.

CALVIN: Hmmmm.

STEVE: Bullshit. Art. Invest in art. Hockney, Brill, Giacometti, Warhol.

DAVID: Hmmmm.

AMY: Hmmmm.

DAVID: Do I have to give my agent 10 percent?

STEVE: You give your agent 10 percent?

CALVIN: You have an agent?

Foreign markets.
Foreign rights. Art.

Heterosexual love.
Heterosexual infidelity.
Homosexual love.

I'M EXHAUSTED.

I don't start writing a novel or novella.

However, I do think about becoming a volunteer at Women for Women International.

SIX

MA, MOM, MOTHER, BEA—
Florida—Part 1

I visit my mom down in Tamarac, Florida, for Mother's Day weekend. She calls it a "villa." This is not a villa. It's a large apartment, attached to another large apartment, with the layout being exactly the same. A selling point—you say "villa," it gives it more of a mystique. I prefer to call it Varicose Village. I have never in my life seen as many ugly strip malls as I have in one community, each one outdoing itself by exuding less personality than the next. Putrid. Slabs of flat concrete painted drab colors, like putty, or hospital green, or my favorite—calamine pink. This is not a place I will retire to if in fact I ever decide to retire. How do you retire from writing? Do you just shut down the laptop and say, "Okay, done," or do you put down the ballpoint pen and say, "Bye-bye. I'm into pencils now!"

I WILL NOT BE RETIRING TO FLORIDA.

Perhaps Aix-en-Provence, or Belize, or San Miguel, or Costa Rica, but, most definitely, not Florida.

I wake up at 3:00 AM, and as I wander out of the "extra bedroom–slash–TV room," I catch my mother, out of the corner of my eye, sitting in the den. She is all dressed. I sit down next to her on the couch. We don't say anything for a few minutes; then she turns to me:

"When they let him out of heaven, he'll come back to me."

"Him" is my dad. He died a few years ago. Logic tells me he will not be coming back to her. Logic tells me that he most definitely would have come back to her if he had gone to the supermarket, or the golf course, or the bagel joint. He would have gone out for about an hour, hour and a half, and most definitely, without question, come back to her. She knows he's dead. This she does know.

She confuses my brother with him on occasion. "I want to divorce him. He's mean, and I want to divorce him." My brother has taken over my mom's finances—primarily because she hasn't a clue that when you withdraw money, you need to deduct that amount from your checkbook, or remember that you've taken money out. For a time she thought someone was depleting her account, as in "I'm being robbed." She forgets to deduct. She forgets to subtract. She forgets, on occasion, that Dad died and the person she wants to divorce is her son.

She forgets so much these days. She hasn't a clue that when it gets dark late in the day, that's called night. Or evening. Growing up, she would always say, "Dinner is not the same as supper, night is not the same as evening." Now she doesn't remember night from day, dinner from supper, evening from night.

It's all a blur to her.

I have a photo of my mom on my refrigerator. It was taken when she was in her early twenties, and she was newly married. She was absolutely, unbelievably beautiful. She looked just like a movie star. She was sexy and stunning and dangerous and oh, god . . . looking at her face, looking in her eyes, you can tell that she didn't want to have children. She didn't want to take care of anyone. Maybe I can see it in her eyes; maybe you wouldn't be able to. Maybe I know too much and have heard too much and so when I see her in these photos where she looks gorgeous, and has such a presence, I see what she really wanted. She wanted to be taken care of, with not a care in the world. She didn't want to raise kids and move to Long Island and live in a suburb where every single house was exactly the same. She had dreams of being an artist. Back then most women tucked their dreams away in a drawer, pushed to the side next to other dreams, aspirations, and lingerie. I look at my mom in that photo and I see a

woman . . . myself. I do—I see myself. Glimpses, anyway—the
selfishness, the fears, and that spark of anger, the wanting to
be taken care of, the not wanting to take care of anyone.
I CAN SEE ME IN HER EYES, IN THAT PHOTO.

*On my last trip to Florida, I had to tell her that she couldn't,
she wouldn't, be driving anymore. She stood in the doorway of
her bathroom, and she cried.* Her license expired. Ten years
expired. It baffles me that she didn't renew it. She seemed very
much aware ten years ago. She played golf and mah-jongg
and traveled, and she knew the difference between a credit
card and a debit card . . . and she would have never let milk
go sour in the fridge. She would have never left the iron on
all day long. She would have never let flowers sit in a vase in
dirty, smelly, mildewed water on the glass-top coffee table in
the living room. She would have never peed on the floor and
covered her mouth in absolute horror that she had no control
over her bladder, let alone anyone or anything else. She would
have never said, *"When they let him out of heaven, he'll come
back to me,"* because my mother never believed in heaven. We
were either going to hell, or we were going shopping. Trust me,
we were never going to heaven.

She has fits, bursts of anger. She was always somewhat angry.
And I, of course, always thought she was almighty powerful.
What I realize now, in my infinite wisdom, is that I mistook
her bullying and screaming and yelling . . . for power. The
louder she was, the more powerful I believed she was. Now
when she screams and yells and has fits of great rage, I see
her as a lonely, scared woman who is facing the last act with
great resentment. Her neurologist tells me that most folks

who are in some stage of dementia are filled with great rage and irritability and react impulsively. *I wonder to myself if my mother has had dementia her entire life. She has always been a version of who she is now.*

I don't long for the mother I used to have. That woman was selfish and brutal and competitive and unforgiving. That woman was very self-indulgent. The woman I speak to now is so much more KIND and GENTLE and FRAGILE. She looks at me with great appreciation. When I called to tell her that I would be visiting her, she said, "Thank you for being so very kind to me. I can't tell you what that means." She needs me now. She never needed me before. I was always trying to get her to love me in ways that probably felt deeply uncomfortable for her.

She tells me on this visit that she didn't want to have two

children. Then she takes my hand and tells me that she loves me.

I know both to be true.

"When they let him out of heaven, he'll come back to me."

I tell her that Daddy died. He's not coming back. I make a joke about how it's not like he's in prison and serving time, and soon they'll let him out for good behavior. She laughs.

I have always, regardless of where we were in our relationship, loved my mother's laugh. Along with her stunning looks, it was the one thing about her that I wanted to inherit.

"He will," she says with great conviction, "come back for me. And I will be here"—stroking the couch with her acrylic nails—"right here waiting."

I nod. I mean, really, what do you say? We sit quietly, my head resting on her shoulder.

Then, much to my surprise, she asks me what I'm doing up in the middle of the night. For a moment she seems completely alert, completely aware. I think to myself, "She knows it's the middle of the night—that's a good sign." I tell her I'm menopausal.

"MENOPAUSE?" SHE ASKS.

"YES," I ANSWER.

"But you're only twelve."

This is the photo of my mom

that is on my refrigerator.

SEVEN

THANK Y⊙U, FUCK Y⊙U,

a.k.a. fuck you very much

Sometimes, in the middle of the night, while I'm staring up at the ceiling because I'm too exhausted to get up out of bed BECAUSE I HAVEN'T SLEPT STRAIGHT THROUGH A NIGHT IN ALMOST FIVE YEARS, I think about all the causes and organizations and department stores I would like to donate money to.

Let me list them in order of preference:

V-Day

Feminist.com

Women for Women International

Save Darfur

Safe Haven, Inc.

ASPCA

MoMA

CARE

Barneys New York

Bergdorf Goodman

Henri Bendel

The Omega Institute

NPR

Obama for America

Himalayan Institute

The Emerson Inn and Spa

New Age Health Spa

Amnesty International

NYWIFT (New York Women in Film & Television)

The Women's Media Center

Alcoholics Anonymous

Veterans for Veterinarians

Bowling for Dollars

And last but not least:

THE NEW YORK STATE LOTTERY
('cause all you need is a dollar and a dream . . .)

As I lie in bed I think about joining the Peace Corps or Habitat for Humanity (or Brad Pitt's new post-Katrina eco-organization, because . . . well, why not), *where I can use my tremendous skills at communication, i.e., screaming at my husband for not cleaning up after himself,* to create a somewhat less messy and more peaceful environment in, say, post-tsunami Malaysia. I know how much my screaming has enabled my dear, sweet, loving, kind, generous husband to declutter his office.

HE RESPONDS BY GIVING ME THE FINGER. And then I respond by giving him the finger. And we do this for about ten, fifteen minutes. And because both of us have arthritis, our fingers curl and our hands gnarl up, and neither one of us can pick up after ourselves for an entire week. My husband tells me that this is called a "self-fulfilled prophecy."

And that, my friends, is where the "Fuck you very much" part comes in from the title of this chapter.

EIGHT

MARRYING GEORGE CLOONEY

Please raise your hand if you have ever had a fantasy of marrying George Clooney.

I have taken a poll among my many curiously deranged, off-balance girlfriends who very often find themselves dancing or, in some cases, swaying to the beat of their own iPod in the middle of the night.

Each one, honest to god, has a similar fantasy. Mine goes like this.

Tossing and turning, more tossing and turning, and more . . . tossing, and more . . . turning.

YOU SLIP OUT OF BED AND FIND YOURSELF STANDING
IN FRONT OF THE BATHROOM VANITY MIRROR: the puffy
droopy eyelids, along with the ever-so-slightly sag in the
jowls—and you can understand on a cellular level how Faye
Dunaway was able to turn herself into a radioactive trout.
FIRST IT WAS THE EYES. Let's pull and tuck them tightly
(adding the glamour of Scotch tape) so that they appear to no
longer be in the center of the face. LET'S TAKE THE NOSE,
which at one time was so perfect and straight, and now expand
the nostrils so they can hide canned goods in case of a nuclear
meltdown. AND NOW THE LIPS—it's always such a tragedy
when the mouth starts to take on the form and shape of a six-
lane freeway. Why, oh, why do we women do this to ourselves?
Really, what is the point? Because we want to get hired as the
ingénue, the sexy hot babe. *Hey, I've got news for you—we*

are sexy hot women, but we're all botoxing ourselves into

non-expression frenzy mode. I mean, really—what is so sexy

about a shiny forehead that only seems to move when you

jerk your arm?

Back to my fantasy.

I GO INTO A BAR.
There are a few scattered customers. Mostly drunk out of their
gourd, mumbling, wobbling, and peeing in their pants. I order
a Cosmo, straight up, which really means cranberry juice with
a twist of lime. I get up from my bar stool and saunter over to
the jukebox. I play Laura Nyro and Rickie Lee Jones. I, for
one, want to hear women sing about rejection and pain and

unrequited love and abortion and guys named Chuck E. who, yes, are in love.

And then he walks in.

Makes himself comfortable at the end of the bar. Orders a beer. Fiddles with his brand-new, sleek, black, sexy iPhone. He looks at me. I look at him. He looks at me again. I mouth, "Hey . . . want my number?" in perfect Italian. He looks at me in his Clooney kind of way, eyebrows tilting up, eyes looking down . . . a smirk . . . he nods. Then he slides the iPhone ever so gracefully—landing right in front of me. I punch in my ten-digit number and add a smiley face with a wink, sliding it right back to him.

"Hey," he says, "you have three 7s in your number. That's lucky."

"Yeah," I say. "Yeah. That's me, Ms. Very, Very Lucky."

NINE MONTHS TO THE DAY I GIVE BIRTH TO OUR FIRST CHILD, WHOM WE NAME DOLORES CLAIBORNE CLOONEY. She dies three days later under mysterious circumstances. Then I fall into a coma. And stay in a vegetative state for eight years. The only people who seem to visit me on a regular basis are Robert and Mary Schindler, Terri Schiavo's parents, who petition to adopt me. I vaguely remember hearing someone—possibly a nurse or an attendant—saying that George thanked me at an Oscar ceremony. He didn't mention me by name, but he did refer to me as *"his coma girl."*

Boy George releases a single that same year, *"Coma, Coma, Coma, Coma Girl,"* and experiences a huge comeback post-jail.

I end up on the cover of *Time* magazine, as "Vegetative Person of the Year."

I wake up from my coma; George and I inevitably divorce. Amicably. I open a fast-food vegan restaurant, called Vegetative Taste, with a drive-through for hybrids only. It becomes a franchise, and I am awarded the Nobel Prize.

I AM JARRED BY THE SOUND OF AN ALARM CLOCK.

My husband, upon waking, turns to me: "What's with the Scotch tape?"

He cannot relate at all to my fantasy life with George.

NINE

O MAGAZINE OH MAGAZINES OH GOD . . . MAGAZINES

I read magazines when I can't sleep.
(**FYI**: I have a pile of magazines under my night table, some of which date back to 1990, '91, '92. There are more dead people under my night table than there are in Montefiore cemetery.)

Vanity Fair, Travel & Leisure, Body & Soul, Good Housekeeping, Town & Country, Yoga International, Gourmet, New York Magazine, The New Yorker, People, Us, Elle, Star, Vogue, Harper's, Glamour, More, Departures, Time, Newsweek, Entertainment Weekly, Rolling Stone, Playboy (for

the interviews), *Ms.*, *Mother Jones*, *National Geographic* (for
the photos), *Martha Stewart Living*, *Simple Living*, *Country
Living*, *Incarcerated Living*, *Urban Living*, *Suburban Living*,
Just Plain Living, *Mountain Living*, *Living Buddhism*, *The Art
of Living*, *Shambala*, *Tricycle*, *Utne*, *A Dog's Life*, *A Man's
Life*, *Women and Co.*, *Esquire*, *Architectural Digest*, *Readers
Digest*, *Digestion & Colon Cleansing*, *Women in Film*, *Men
in Film*, *Teenagers Who Want to Be in Film*, *Film Journal*,
Writers' Journal, *Journey into the Unknown*, *Mademoiselle*,
Money, *Forbes*, *Fortune*, *SpaFinder*, *Relevant Times*, *Irrelevant
Times*, *TV Guide* . . . and the mother of all magazines:

O MAGAZINE.

And why exactly am I giving it that distinction—the mother
of all magazines? Do I really, really like the magazine, does it
really tap into my inner "O" child, do I feel safe and cuddly
and warm when I read it, thumb through it? Is she really,
truly just like me? Or am I afraid to say that it's not even as
good as some, like, say, *Vanity Fair*, or *The New Yorker*, or even
Bitch, which for my money has highly intelligent, relevant
pieces, not to mention a fine selection of films and books and
wonderful critiques?

Maybe the truth is I'm afraid of Oprah. Maybe I'm so fucking
afraid of her that I dare not tell her the truth out of fear that I
will not get an Oprah Book Club approval.

Or maybe . . . just maybe . . .

I really, really love the magazine and I'm just afraid to openly admit that to all my girlfriends who think it's overrated and redundant and hate the fact that she's on the cover every single month and really don't like any of her O picks, especially the cashmere throws that cost an arm and a leg and make us all wonder who other than Oprah herself can afford such an item.

A CONFLICT. Maybe Martha Beck can help me.

TEN

SECRETS &
JUNK DRAWERS

*Fear, guilt, panic, and anxiety not only take hold of me but
also own me, every inch of me, in the middle of the night.*

I am often jarred awake not by good, happy, joyous thoughts
but by doom, despair, gloom, terror, and . . . shame.

As in: *"Ohmigod, what were we thinking?"*

SECRETS.

The ones we've kept. The ones we've spilled. And the hope—
the get-down-on-our-knees-and-pray-to-almighty-god kind of
hope—that the real awful, bad, shut-my-eyes-and-wave-this-
crap-away kind of secrets will never, ever see the light of day.

"I don't care who you are, and I don't care where you live, everyone has a junk drawer. Maybe even two."

That quote came from my mother.

My husband, my WTGK *(wonderful, talented, generous, and kind)* husband, has one huge, massive, disgusting, filthy, hideous junk drawer. Some people in the twelfth and thirteenth centuries would have probably called it a dungeon. Some folks in the late-eighteenth to early nineteenth centuries would have more than likely called it a torture chamber, BUT TODAY IN THE TWENTY-FIRST CENTURY, RIGHT HERE IN AMERICA, MOST FOLKS WOULD CALL IT "A BASEMENT." And for close to fifteen years now, we—my husband and I, since I, through marriage, go under the heading of "accomplice"—have managed to keep that room a genuine, bona fide secret.

Sort of like how a psychopathic homicidal crazy is able to keep "a secret life" down in the cellar from the mother whom he still lives with at the age of forty-two, all while she sits one flight up in the living room watching sitcoms, laughing uproariously while wishing out loud—to anyone she meets—that her son should live in his own apartment with neighbors like Will and Grace and Jack.

I imagine on moist, rainy days their conversations go something like this:

"Honey, what's that smell coming from the basement?"

"WHAT SMELL, MA?"

"You don't smell anything, darling?"

"YOU MEAN MILDEW? WE HADDA LOT OF RAIN LATELY, MA."

"Oh. Yes. How silly of me. Mildew."

Turns out that it isn't mildew after all. And on one fateful day (because he is *so* tired of keeping the "bad, bad" secret), he is caught. What a shock-a-runi that must be for the Mrs. Ma.

And just like with that mother and son, that fateful day arrived for us. It was an act of god, a massive ice storm, that made Ken throw up his hands and say, "Someone has to go to our house, get into the basement, and make sure the pipes don't freeze." I wonder what my face must have looked like, all contorted like that? I can only imagine like a woman who's addicted to crack and has a hypothyroid condition.

I CAN'T POSSIBLY DESCRIBE THE BASEMENT TO YOU. However I describe "the basement," trust me, wouldn't do it justice. I can say it's a cross between the Collyer brothers and hell, but that's not cluttered enough. I could say it's a cross between the underbelly of the New York subway system and van Gogh's studio after he offed his ear, but that's not quite dark and dank and red enough. I could say it's a cross between the damage done by Hurricane Katrina and the tsunami, but that's just not ethical or moral. Let's just say, for argument's sake, it's vile.

In the dictionary, the *ENCARTA WORLD ENGLISH DICTIONARY*, the word vile (adj.) is defined as *"causing disgust and abhorrence; very evil or shameful; extremely unpleasant to experience."* Vile it is.

I asked my **WTGK** husband whom he thought we should call.

"ALAN AND JULIE."

Ohmigod.

"Alan and Julie? Whatdya, nuts? How about calling the fella down the road, the one with the bad eye, you know, the blind eye and that bad hair piece—what about calling him."

"HE'S NOT OUR FRIEND, AND BESIDES, I DON'T WANT HIM IN OUR HOUSE."

"You want A FRIEND in our basement?"

We've gotten rip-roaring drunk with Alan and Julie; we've spit up food in front of each other—my husband has thrown up in their bathroom after being so drunk and so sick that even to this day he doesn't recall the experience. We've consoled each other, we've laughed with and at each other, we've gone months without talking, and then like most people who have an indescribable connection picked up right where we left off, we've fantasized about going to Paris together, but realized we didn't want the French people hating Americans even more than they already do. We've even shared pharmaceutical secrets. And Julie was the person—even before Ken—who I gave the hot-off-the-press very first copy of my novel to. While we were having dinner at the Four Seasons restaurant, I handed her my gleaming new book from Houghton Mifflin— we both screamed—and then ordered froufrou drinks until we were blotto. But there was no way on this earth that I would allow them into our dungeon.

"Please, for god's sake, Ken, can't we just ask the blind man to come over?"

"I'M CALLING ALAN AND JULIE."

"Call the friggin' blind man."

"ALAN AND JULIE."

"Blind man."

"ALAN AND JULIE."

"Blind man."

"ALAN AND JULIE."

"Blind man, blind man, blind man. Please, please, please, please . . . "

And just when it looked like it could go either way, I threw in what could possibly be known as the pièce de résistance: *"I will give you a blow job every day for a year."*

And then there was dead silence for what felt like a couple of days.

"NO, YOU WON'T. WHY ARE YOU LYING ABOUT THAT? YOU KNOW WHAT, BECAUSE YOU JUST LIED ABOUT THAT, YOU HAVE TO CALL ALAN AND JULIE."

Ken handed me the phone. With great shame I called Alan and Julie. Thankfully, it went straight to voice mail. I left a message saying that it was an emergency—we were out of town and we were worried, worried sick, that our pipes were going to freeze, and could they please, please, please go over, and I would completely and utterly understand if they didn't want to associate with us any longer after seeing our basement.

So, I bolted up in the middle of the night: *"Ohmigod, what were we thinking?"* I could not fall back asleep. I was mortified. This big bad horrible secret was about to blow wide open. My husband, Mr. Oh Yeah, I Get Up in the Middle of the Night, was sleeping soundly. He didn't give a shit that we were about to lose our friends to his filth. In his mind all we needed was a new broom, a quick sweep; in my mind we needed a fucking blowtorch and a toxic waste cleaning crew, hazmat suits and all. And let me just say for the record, when you're in the thick of menopause, there are no molehills, only mountains.

That morning, we got a call from Alan—he and Julie were on vacation, but the guy who was taking care of their house would stop by our house on the way to their house ASAP to check on our pipes.

I believe that's called "a save."

The blind man said our pipes didn't freeze.

And someone, whose name starts with the letter **K**, will not be getting any blow jobs for an entire year. I advise him to collect "un-enjoyment."

ELEVEN

OUR LADY OF PERPETUAL SHOPPING

It's really crazy wacky what you can buy online in the middle of the night. Everything from moisturizers (both facial and vaginal) to yachts (both humongous and miniature) to personalized eulogies to a hair follicle from some guy in Minnesota who is selling all his personal (obviously) shit on eBay. It's amazing, really, if you think about it. We no longer even have to leave our home, except of course if we work for a living, and even that's debatable these days, especially with Skype. You can make-believe that you're at work, or at your office, or even stuck in a subway train, but really . . . *surprise!* . . . you're at home, lying in bed, sitting on your couch, relaxing in your Barcalounger, faking everyone out by wearing a shirt and a tie, or a sweater set and pearls and . . . pajama bottoms.

There are websites, I kid you not, where you can have shoes made via an Internet cobbler. They have all sorts of charts and color wheels and styles, from Mary Janes to ballet flats to wooden clogs.

They will help you design, create, and cobble a perfect pair of shoes that you yourself helped create and design and cobble. You send them exact measurements of each foot. Perhaps one foot is longer and wider. Not impossible. After all, in the words of Pema Chödrön, "Imperfection is Perfection." So, every imperfection, every long toe, every short fat toe, every bump, every callous will be measured so precisely so as to coordinate the inner sole and the leather lining down to the corn on your baby toe *(or toes)*. Itsy-teeny double-stitching, multicolored, multilayered leather *(or nonleather if you're a vegan)*, not to mention heels that go from six inches to two inches—from two inches to flats, from round-toed to pointy-toed, from knee-high boots to ankle boots, from sandals to military lace-ups, from leather thongs to Roman lace-ups, from over-the-thigh suede to all-in-one including leather bra and panties.

I forward this website to all my shoe-fanatic friends, and in the subject line I write: "Yay! We can design our own shoes!!!!!"

And I hate to admit this, but most of my shoe-fanatic friends— and there are plenty—find this a complete waste of time. With the exception of one, who is totally into leather, none found this at all appealing.

To me, it's a fucking miracle.

TWELVE

TV MOGUL TIME

THERE IS SO MUCH DRECK ON TELEVISION—MY
HUSBAND CALLS THEM "SHITCOMS." As I lie awake, I can't
help but imagine and concoct, in my very own mind, fabulous
and funny half-hour comedies, and/or one-hour dramatic and
daring TV series, or a combination of both known as

the dramedy.

Here is a sampling of a few of my make-believe Emmy-worthy shows:

LAVENDER DAYS
A one-hour dramedy *(sad, poignant, laugh out loud)* TV series
set in a gay retirement village in Key West, Florida. Two
retired policewomen, having met during a drug sting on
the Lower East Side, own and run the place. And of course,

they're life partners. A cross between *Desperate Housewives* and *Cagney & Lacey.*

I DON'T

A half-hour comedy about a couple who have been married for eighteen glorious years only to find out—via the evening news— that the minister who married them was a complete and utter fraud. So, ta-da . . . they were never legally married. And we watch this "glorious, perfect" marriage unravel right before our eyes. A cross between *Rashomon* and *Everybody Loves Raymond.*

OWNER WANTED

An animated series (or, if on Bravo, a reality series) about a dog, Henry, whose very wealthy and loving owner, Mrs. Myra Glindenfestamin of the Glindenfestamin supermarket chain, passes away, leaving Henry with a massive financial fortune. He sets out to find a new person who will love him and care for him, via an ad in the local newspaper—and boy, oh boy, do folks come out of the animated (or reality) woodwork. It's amazing what people will do for money.

TOUGH TITTIES

HBO or Showtime. (Or AMC, since they're really hot and on the map now.) A one-hour dramatic series: gritty, edgy, down and dirty, tough, and sexy. Females. Boxing. *"Man-olo a Man-olo."* Jennifer Lopez executive-produces.

PET PEEVES

An animated sitcom: ANIMALS IN GROUP THERAPY. The pilot episode is called "Of Mice and Mensches." Tagline: *Lithium—a new leash on life.*

THIRTEEN

WG☉D—
Mom—Part 2

My mom is Jewish, which on a not-so-deep profound level explains why, when I wake up in the middle of the night, I am filled with fear, doubt, guilt, and shame. And, of course, being a Buddhist, I am determined to transform all that negativity into . . . COLD HARD CASH.

These days my mom talks to Jesus in the middle of the night. She has a laminated "photo" of him on her nightstand and has—for no apparent, explainable reason—fallen head over heels for him.

She tells me she loves Jesus. I ask her if she has become a Jew for Jesus. She shakes her head, "No, of course not. But I love him."

I am visiting her in New Mexico, where we have recently moved her from Florida into an adult "CARE" community with "AMENITIES"—a tiered assisted-living community. My brother lives about fifteen minutes away. That's the good and bad news. Good for her; very, very bad for him. Right now she's in the midtier of what's called "INDEPENDENT LIVING." Every morning and every evening a "WELLNESS TECHNICIAN" (formerly known as a nurse) comes in, gives her all her pills, puts drops in her eyes; takes her blood pressure, checks on her shingles—applying a soothing cream that alleviates the pain and burning from the shingles—and, every so often, will escort her down to the dining room, where she will find someone sitting alone and *(hopefully, with a capital H)* she will join them. My mom is not a joiner. She prefers to be invited and then say no. She's as stubborn and contrary as the day is long.

FOR THE RECORD, MY MOM, MY PARENTS WERE NOT RELIGIOUS PEOPLE. We were occasional Jews, as in: we went to shul on the occasional Jewish holidays, the occasional bar or bat mitzvah, and on the sad occasion of a funeral. *But we were not lighting candles on Friday nights, or changing the china and silverware from kosher to nonkosher and back to kosher.* And when my mother said (very often) that god was going to punish us, she was in fact referring to my father.

Since my dad's death, my mother has been trying to "FIND HIM." His death was sudden and unexpected. You can tell by looking at her that she is completely tormented by his "DISAPPEARANCE," as she often refers to it.

I am staying in the guest room, right next to her bedroom. When I wake up in the middle of the night due to severe hot flashes (my mother keeps the apartment at a cool eighty-eight degrees), I hear her talking to Jesus:

"You seem like such a nice, kind fella. You're young, good-looking—a little unkempt, but very kind. I like that you're kind—I like that you use your hands a lot when you talk, and you seem very smart, and I'm wondering if you saw my Sam up in heaven. Sam is my husband, and I think he needs to come home now; he's probably a little confused—he wasn't expecting to leave Florida, I think maybe there's been a mistake. Maybe you were supposed to take the fella that lived down the road from us—I forget his name, Manny, Morrie . . . it'll come back to me—he was very old and he couldn't walk, he used a walker, and he had a very bad burn by the side of his head, he was much more fragile, *so maybe you made a mistake, taking my Sam instead of that fella,* what's-his-name. He seems ready. So, maybe you can bring my husband home, and you can stay with us in our guest room—we have a nice room for you. It has a TV, not so big, but it has a remote, so you can watch TV from the bed and change all the channels, and I think, but I'm not sure, that it even has a Spanish station. You can watch the news so you know what's going on all day long. PLEASE BRING SAM HOME TO ME. He's tall and thin, and maybe isn't eating so well right now, so he might be thinner, and he's very handsome. *Oh, my god, he's so handsome.* The first time I saw him, he took my breath away. I, of course, was wearing a red two-piece bathing suit,

and I made his heart stop. But he made mine pound. Thank you, Jesus. Oh, and the fella's name is Morris. *Please, take him and return Sam. We'll call it a trade. You're allowed to trade—you're Jesus."*

My Mom and Dad
On the back of this photo in my
mom's handwriting, it reads:
"Very Shameful (but swell)"

FOURTEEN

HIT THE ROAD, JACK

A young girl stands at the exit ramp at the intersection of I-25 North and Paseo del Norte.

She stands—shivering in the cold. Wearing jeans that are frayed and ripped at the knees, a jacket that is a good, decent spring weather jacket, not a winter-weather "with the hint of a blizzard passing through" jacket. She is holding up a sign—which for my money is one of the funniest, most poignant and clever signs I have ever seen being held up at any exit or entrance ramp anywhere for that matter:

STRANDED
BECAUSE OF
BAD TASTE IN MEN.

I hand her a crisp five-dollar bill, the only bill that I have in my wallet, and tell her, HEY, WE'VE ALL BEEN THERE, AND THE ONES WHO TELL YOU THEY HAVEN'T ARE COMPLETELY FULL OF SHIT. I don't know one woman who hasn't been stranded by someone somewhere in the world. Hey, I've been stranded in my own home.

She is cute, with a dazzling smile and a wacky sort of hairstyle that matches her very eclectic taste in clothes. I can't imagine what she must've done to have some guy dump her, leaving her hitching and stranded on I-25.

I ask my mom—oh, wise one with dementia—and she says to me, *"Sometimes if you breathe wrong, they toss you out. I hope she finds a nice neurosurgeon, and has a baby and forgets about this fucking asshole who made her stand out in the freezing cold."*

Immediately upon waking in the middle of the night, I think about the girl and really, deeply hope and pray that she's okay. She had such an abundance of spunk. And I sincerely hope that whoever stranded her had a major blowout and is now standing at the entrance ramp in East Bumbfuck, Anywhere, USA, with a sign that reads:

I AM A SCHMUCK

Just leave me stranded.

I deserve it.

FIFTEEN

GREAT SEX

My husband and I have great sex in the middle of the night, somewhere between three and four in the morning. I have been told that is often considered the *"enlightened hour."*

Enlightened is not the first adjective on my list:

romantic, passionate, sexy, hot, wet . . . color-me-crazy-delirious

comes to mind first.

Je ne sais quoi?

SIXTEEN

SCARY, SCARY NIGHT

This is a very long story with which I will not bore you with all the little, tiny minutiae. Suffice it to say, we are in the middle of the rain forest in a very secluded, remote hotel, and I wake up in the middle of the night scared shitless that some very scary people—*Children of the Corn*–type people, covered in full body tattoos—will be coming after us, since I inadvertently (under paranoid, emotional pressure) gave them the name and exact address of this (very, very remote) hotel.

This scares me.

I am deeply worried that they will come to our hotel and murder us.

I don't wake up Ken.

HE DOESN'T WORRY ABOUT STUFF LIKE THIS.

As I lie awake, I think about all the other stuff I worry about when I can't sleep (this is not in any particular order):

MONEY (not having enough, having too much and giving it away, pissing it away, good investments, bad investments, and, of course, the big, big worry: identity and PIN theft)

WRITING (as in "blocked")

WORK (as in "very blocked")

AGING (self-explanatory; scroll to "Sagging breasts")

MY CAT, WISHES (he's very old and frail and has kidney problems)

MY HUSBAND, KEN *(let me pin this down to just three: I worry that he will die in a car accident, that he will be paralyzed from the neck down from that car accident, that he will become incontinent)*

MY MOM, BEA *(she's old and has dementia; scroll up to "My cat, Wishes")*

FIRES (any fire, anywhere, particularly in my house)

FLOODS (ditto)

STORMS (ice, snow, other . . .)

DRIVING IN BAD WEATHER (I worry that the windshield wipers will stop working)

DRIVING IN GOOD WEATHER (I worry about other people driving)

LIP-LINES (mine)

SAGGING BREASTS (scroll up to "Aging"; nipple lines, which *no one,* by the way, is discussing, and this deeply worries me)

DEMENTIA (if I'm forgetting now, what the fuck will I remember in forty plus years from now)

GROWING OLD AND BEING ALONE (or being alone and growing old)

CANCER (I worry a lot about this—sometimes I can go from feeling completely healthy to being riddled with cancer in thirty seconds flat. I can actually feel the cancer growing in my body, which is part and parcel of having menopause and being a hypochondriac—that's called a meno-chondriac)

LEUKEMIA (not so much, but still)

TERRORIST ATTACKS (I worry that the bridges and tunnels and tolls and freeways/highways and Madison Avenue will be blown up)

PLANE CRASHES (I usually start feeling twinges of panic a few nights before I actually get on a plane, worrying that I will not have enough Valium preflight)

BRAIN ANEURYSM (no, they're not cluster headaches)

NERVOUS BREAKDOWNS (again, self-explanatory)

And of course . . .
Death (as in mine,
or anyone else's).

SEVENTEEN

MA BELL—
Mom—Part 3

"Hello."

"Amy?"
"Ma?"

"Amy, I need you to buy me a ticket to get home."
"Ma, it's four in the morning."

"Whatdya talking about, it's four in the afternoon."
"Ma, trust me, it's the middle of the night."

"Not here. Here it's daytime."
"Ma, it's two hours earlier where you are, so, it's what, two in the morning."

"I just had lunch."
"I doubt that."

*"Why do you always have to argue with me, I just had lunch,
I ate with that crazy woman, Gert, you know, the woman
with Alzheimer's. She and I had soup and some crackers
and you know, I forgot to tell you, she steals. Yes, she steals.
She stole a whole basket of crackers and shoved them in her
purse. She's a very unstable person. A criminal type."*

"Ma, I doubt she's a criminal. You steal crackers—I've
seen you."

*"Sure. You see me steal. What the hell are you talking about?
When did you ever see me steal?"*

"Last week, when I visited with you."

*"Last week? You visited me last week? You're dreaming, you
know that. When did you visit me last week?"*

"Ma, I moved you to New Mexico; we came from Florida."

"I want to go home now. I don't like it here."

"Can we talk about this in the morning?"

*"No. I want to talk about it now. You all seem to think if I don't
talk about it, it'll go away. I want to get the hell out of here
and go home and sleep in my own bed."*

"Ma, you *are* sleeping in your own bed. You have all new
furniture."

"I didn't pick it out. This isn't my taste. I have good taste."

"Ma, you love the furniture—you said you loved the furniture."

*"I lied. It's too much clutter. Jews don't clutter. Goys clutter.
You ever see what a goy does to a Christmas tree, for Christ's
sake? It's got more shit on it, dangling balls and confetti.*

This isn't my bed. This isn't my furniture. My bed and my furniture are in Florida, in my house."

"You have to stay in New Mexico."

"Says who?"

"Says me."

"And you are?"

"I'm your daughter."

"But you're not god. God didn't tell me to stay. I don't listen to you. I listen to god."

"Ma?"

"Yeah?"

"You have a contingency plan—a plan B?"

"What's a plan B?"

"You know, in case something doesn't work out. You need a fallback plan."

"Well, that sounds pretty negative if you ask me—a fallback plan? Sounds like you're giving up before you even get started."

"Ma, why're you so contrary? Why is it if I say blue, you say teal; if I say magenta, you say cranberry . . . can't we agree on anything at this ungodly hour?"

"And when is it a godly hour?"

"Well, I'd say after 10:00 AM, that's usually a very godly hour."

"Sure, if god were a prima dona that would be a good time to get in touch. My god, the one I pray to and talk to and cry to, my god, he gets up at four in the morning. He doesn't waste a fucking moment. You need something, boom, he's there, done, taken care of. Your god sounds lazy and irresponsible."

"Okay, so let me get this straight, you want to go home to Florida and be in your home with your furniture, and you want god—your god—to help make all the travel arrangements?"

"Yes. My god."

"Ma, please, hang up and call 411 and see if you can get a listing for god, that's g-o-d, and call him."

"What's 411?"

"Information, Ma."

"I don't need information. I have too much information. That's why I can't think straight. I'm tired now."

CLICK.

DIRTY, DIRTY LAUNDRY

This game is called "Sibling Pathology"—a cross between
Monopoly (the 2008 Elite version) and Poker—where one
sibling ends up with all the "executor power."

I sit at my computer at three in the morning, and this is
what I'm doing. I'm googling family-estate planning, estate
planning, estranged siblings, siblings and dementia, siblings
and dementia and eldercare, power of attorney, sibling rivalry,
hitmen, Vegas weekend getaways all-inclusive, and lawyers for
siblings who no longer speak to each other.

THERE ARE THOUSANDS AND THOUSANDS OF SITES THAT
DEAL WITH THIS KIND OF STUFF.

My brother flat out refuses to reimburse me for money I spent on my mom (traveling, visiting, helping move her) even though it was in fact his idea—this reimbursement thing— in the first place.

I am absolutely floored by his refusal,

which by the way came in the form of an email in ALL CAPS so as to make his point that he was screaming LOUDLY at me, so I understood that *he meant business.* He was adamant that he himself would *never, ever, ever,* EVER ask to be reimbursed because he is a selfless, loving, generous son, and I am a selfish, irresponsible daughter. But it all goes under the umbrella of "history." This is not the first time, and most certainly will not be the last time, that my brother and I have had some form of confrontation WITHOUT ACTUALLY CONFRONTING EACH OTHER. My brother is just like my father, and this is in fact a piece of the family dynamic, which was passed down through my father and my mother, which my brother and I both own a piece of, and I will not bore you with it, except to say that in one way or another it has always been about MONEY. Always. It's as familiar a story as any family drama and, my guess, no more or less dysfunctional. Although, I might stand corrected on that.

I SIT AT MY COMPUTER FEVERISHLY GOOGLING.

I am instantly struck by one particular site, the *Christian Index,* which promises to restore any and all broken relationships, but first you must send them a donation and then you can get a login name and password.

I decide to pass.

Some interesting tidbits I find in my search:
1) IF A PERSON DIES WITHOUT A WILL, THAT IS CALLED AN INTESTATE. I had absolutely no idea. That's called dying intestate, which sounds very much like someone dying right smack in between two states, like, let's say, Pennsylvania and Jersey.

2) THE BABY-BOOMER GENERATION IS MORE LITIGIOUS THAN ANY OTHER GENERATION. That's called greed. More wills and estates are now challenged by what is now called "the hurt feelings clause": "Why didn't Mom give me as much as my sister (brother)?" I call that one typical of my generation.

3) THERE IS ALSO THE EXISTENCE OF UNDUE INFLUENCE—THIS IS WHEN SOMEONE FORCES OR COERCES THE "TESTATOR" TO SIGN A NEW WILL, WHICH MORE THAN LIKELY HAS BEEN ALTERED TO SUIT THE VERY PERSON FORCING THE SIGNATURE. That, too, goes under greed, or possibly nasty, and very fucking cruel behavior. Apparently this kind of thing is going on more and more now, the altering of wills. I am not surprised. I know folks (not very well, though) who would sooner boil their siblings in hot water than see to it that they get their fair share of a will or estate. I know people who have taken every single piece of jewelry and artwork from their parent's home so that their relatives don't have a single memento. I know people who know people who have moved in the middle of the night with a U-Haul attached to their BMW SUV filled with furniture and paintings and Schwinn bicycles so that their siblings are left out to dry.

As I scroll through these stories, testimonials, experiences, I
say out loud to no one in particular: Aha. Sibling rivalry hell.

IN MY FAMILY YOU DON'T MAKE WAVES—you talk about
everyone behind their back, you stab them in their heart,
you act as if you haven't, you hear from all the relatives that
in fact everyone is talking about you *and* everyone else for
that matter, and you make—or attempt to make—amends
but, god forbid, no waves. And just in case you don't know
this, please—jot this down, the reason there were no waves,
my family doesn't swim. They wade. They spend a gazillion
dollars on bathing suits and cabana sets, hats and sunglasses,
and last but not least: waterproof and sweatproof sunblock
lotion with 187 SPF UVA UVB (whatever that all means), but
they never, ever go swimming. THEY WADE.

I decide to become a Superwoman heroine now, fighting off
sibling injustice and bullshit with both my tongue and my
weapon of choice: the mighty pen—and, of course, Google.
I have a (fake wash-off) tattoo strategically placed on my
shoulder:

MAKE WAVES, NOT LOVE.

I am determined. I am armed. I am a woman on a mission.

MY FRIENDS GATHER AROUND AND WE DO A SPECIAL SUFI
DRUM DANCE, CALLING FORTH THE REIMBURSEMENT
GODS AND DEITIES. We dance for hours and hours. My feet
hurt. I have bunions. We eat salsa and pita chips until we

all feel like vomiting. A special reimbursement prayer is put forth into the universe. I send my brother another email. He refuses, tells me in no uncertain terms to go fuck myself. I am very gently reminded by Sufi princess Ana-na-na-na that reimbursement prayer dances aren't always foolproof. I very gently remind her that she should have mentioned this before my feet swelled two sizes and preferably before she pocketed the two hundred and eighty in cash.

I decide it's time for me to distance myself from my "blood" clan and devote the remaining waking moments to becoming a Christian Index member—complete with a dental plan and a metro card giveaway.

AT PEACE IN MY TUB IN THE MIDDLE OF THE NIGHT

Ah, yes.

TWENTY

BITTER WITH A SIDE OF FRIES

My husband and I have a rip-roaring, all-out-screaming

"at the top of my lungs" fight in the middle of the night.
He said something earlier in the evening that I can't seem to
shake off. So, I wake him. I push him and push him . . . and
push him . . . literally, as in a shove.

"HEY," he says, all groggy. *"What the fuck are you doing?"*

I proceed to tell him that I felt very unsupported by him, and
that he should have stood up for me. And I just want to shove
him straight into the wall and make him bleed.

He looks at me as if I took a dose of crazy pills. He props
himself up and stares. *"What the fuck are you talking about?"*

I rant and rave. I rant and rave. A complete, all-out nut dance.
I get out of bed, using both my hands and both my arms in
perfect unison to show how deeply troubled and upset I am by
his . . . his . . . his lack of support.

"YEAH. SO. I DIDN'T LIKE THE PASTA," he says to me.
"IT WASN'T AL DENTE."

I can't even look at him. I go into the living room and sit on
the couch. I stare up at the fireplace—the beautiful painting
that hangs above it, the wonderful pieces of art that line up
perfectly on top of the mantel, the candlestick holders that
are a mixture of gold and copper—and think about how
beautifully I decorated the house, with all my perfect little
touches here and there, and then I wonder out loud, very, very
out loud: How you can marry someone, be with someone close
to fifteen years, and never, ever really know them.

He screams from the bedroom, "FINE—YOU'RE RIGHT.
FUCKING SHOOT ME."

See that. An apology . . .
he knows he's wrong.

TWENTY-ONE

THE BIPOLAR EXPRESS

I am on 25mg of Zoloft. It was about two years ago that

I was driving on Route 80 and had a sudden urge to

drive straight into the median. It felt almost out of body.
Like I no longer had any control over this panic, this sadness,
this overwhelming desire to smash myself to little tiny bits, not
to mention total my car. I call my doctor, who immediately
says, "MENOPAUSE. It's all connected to menopause. I can't
tell you how many women are feeling the same way you
are. Wanting to drive their cars off the freeway." To which
I respond, "MAYBE YOU OUGHTTA OPEN UP A DRIVING
SCHOOL." He laughs. *His laugh irritates me.* It's grating. Like
chalk on a blackboard. Or more specifically like that weird,
unnerving, crazy laugh track in a carnival House of Mirrors.
I don't have patience for it, or him, or for any other woman

who is having vehicular problems. He prescribes Zoloft, 25mg, the pediatric dose. I wonder what that means. Is he saying *I'm giving you the lowest dose because you don't need to be medicated*, or is he saying *I'm giving you the lowest dose because you're an immature, unruly girl-child.* I don't know what he means when he says *I want you to take the pediatric dose.* This sticks with me.

So, I call him again . . . well, that's not true. I don't *call him* call him . . . I make-believe imagine calling him. I imagine dialing his number while I'm lying on my couch in the middle of the night staring up at the ceiling fan as it spins ever so slowly as to make me nauseated. I imagine that he answers his phone and I say, *Hey, did you give me this dosage because I'm acting like a child, or because the lowest dose is in fact going to take the edge off.* Then he tells me, in my imaginary phone conversation, that he gave me the lowest dose because I am quite mature and in fact healthier than most of his patients. I am relieved. And I figure while I have him on this call, and god knows how difficult it is to actually get him to take a call after hours, I ask him if he thinks the headaches I'm experiencing could possibly be a brain tumor. He asks me if the swiggles I'm seeing are color-coded or in fact just bolts— quick bolts that race before my eyes. I tell him I'm not sure if they're in color. Maybe. Maybe they're a bunch of bright colors that may be blinding me. There's a moment of silence, and then he says, *You would know if you had a brain tumor, your head would be throbbing unbearably, and you wouldn't be able to blink your eyes without there being excruciating pain.* I tell him that I don't feel any of those things, so I can rule out brain tumor. I AM RELIEVED. I have one more inquiry—I ask about the pain in my stomach and wonder if he thinks maybe I have an ulcer or possibly irritable bowel syndrome.

He ups the dosage to 50mg. Hmmmm. I ask him, What kind of dose is that—he says a prepubescent adolescent dose. To which I say, Oh I get it, you're not really a doctor, you just play one on my make-believe TV.

How is it I can be so quick-witted on these imaginary phone calls?

TWENTY-TWO

RAGTIME

The clock reads 2:34 AM.

I am determined to fall back asleep. Determined. I am determined to fall back asleep without any help from any sleep enhancement drugs—just plain old will and strength.

THE CLOCK NOW READS 3:47 AM.

Fuck it.

I turn on the light. Dim, very dim, as to not disturb my husband, who is sound asleep and snoring. I would like for you to envision what I now see as I roll on my side to grab a magazine, a magazine that is on his side of the bed because he wanted to see the photos of Brad and Angelina.

An *eye mask, earplugs, a lip-drool thing* that looks a bit like Bell's palsy, and my favorite part of this whole nighttime sleep ritual: what my husband likes to refer to as a PENIS RAG—a piece of toilet paper wrapped around his penis. This is what he does after he pees in the middle of the night. He pees. He wraps. He comes back to bed, all while wearing the eye mask.

There is a trail of toilet paper from the bathroom to the bedroom. I kid you not.

While having breakfast, I hand my husband a paper towel. He reminds me, in a semilecture sort of way, that I need to be more "green," more conscientious, more eco-friendly, more aware of the environment—I should start using "linen" napkins, because paper napkins, paper towels, paper anything is a waste. I am wasteful, and I need to be more eco-aware.

I tell him that he's absolutely 100 percent right. Yes, I am wasteful; yes, I need to be more eco-friendly. I can tell by the way he tilts his head and sips his coffee that he feels thunderously victorious. I give him his moment in the sun. I let him bask. And then I do something I never, ever think in a million years I would do. I say nothing.

NOTHING. NOT A WORD. I KNOW THAT ACTIONS— ACTIONS—SPEAK MUCH LOUDER THAN WORDS.

In the middle of the night, when Ken gets up to pee, folded ever so perfectly over the toilet-paper holder, is a linen napkin.

And because I am up at this ungodly hour, sitting at my computer, I can hear him—somewhat faint, but definitely irritated:

"Smartass."

TRAILER PARKS & TORNADOES

*That is both a question and
an observation.*

*This is something that truly,
truly baffles me.*

Has anyone else taken notice?

*I understand it all theoretically,
I do. It's just . . .*

WHELMED (NOT OVER, NOT UNDER)

I am at my computer, answering emails in the middle of the night—emails that I've saved, that I didn't respond to in the afternoon. For whatever reason, I often feel if I start answering emails in the afternoon, then my friends will know that I am not working on my book. But, if I write emails in the middle of the night, then they'll think I've written all day.

IT'S ALL A BIG LIE.

I've had writer's block for close to four years. Everyone who knows me knows this. So I don't know what the big fucking secret is. Except, as you can

tell, it's pathological. As I go through "unanswered" emails—a pop-up IM from a friend, who is also awake in the middle of the night, and she asks me in big, bold letters ARE YOU UP? I respond, *yeah, i'm up* (all lowercase). In the next email, again, in big bold letters: ARE YOU AFRAID OF DEATH? I don't know what she means by this. I wonder, to myself, *Does she mean in general am I afraid of death,* or is she asking me because she in fact is a stalker-slash-murderer and about to kill me through the Internet. I've seen that movie—it starred Denise Richards; everyone gets murdered as soon as they hit the reply button on their computer. I send back a very quick answer: *"Why you asking?"* Again, in big bold letters, "BECAUSE I AM SCARED OF DEATH. I THINK ABOUT IT ALL THE TIME, ESPECIALLY NOW, WHEN I CAN'T SLEEP." I wonder if her caps lock key is broken, or if she's having a nervous breakdown. I've also seen that movie, a Lifetime TV movie, starring Veronica Hamel.

I tell her that I'm not afraid of death per se; I'm more afraid of being forgotten. I'm afraid when I die no one will come to my funeral, that I will be found out, that someone will go through all my drawers and closets and find out that I was such a clutter pig, and that people will talk bad about me, especially now that I'm dead—they'll talk even LOUDER behind my back—that my life will end up a sham and all the private, emotional stuff that I took to my grave will be revealed, and any and all secrets that I told someone will come back to haunt me (or post-haunt me), and that I'll become a huge success posthumously, and will win all sorts of writing prizes, and a library or department store will be built in my honor, and a hamburger will be named after me, the Amy "With Everything Except Mayonnaise" Burger.

That I'm not really afraid of the dying part of death, I'm much more afraid of the post-effect part of it.

She sends me back an email: SOUNDS LIKE YOU'RE A REAL CONTROL FREAK.

hey, bitchface, you're the one who asked me, okay. i was pretty fucking happy minding my own business, not thinking about death, okay??????

TESTY.

freak.

OH I'M SHAKING—OOOOOOOOHHHHHHH. SHAKING.

very mature. love the emphasis on the oh.

I DON'T WANT TO BE YOIR FRIEND ANYMORE.

not yoir. your. get off the fucking caps lock and use your spell-check. fine. die. see if i care. see if I come to your funeral. see if I give a shit. do not IM me again in the middle of the night, you've woken up my entire family with your loud stupid CAPS. go away....

FUCK YOU, FUCK YOU, FUCK YOU!!!!!!

bye-bye. going off line now.

I lose sleep.
I lose friends.
But I will have a hamburger named after me.

TWENTY-FIVE

HELLO DARKNESS, MY OLD FRIEND

It's called coming to a crossroads. You don't know whether to turn left or right.

HERE'S THE ROAD MAP:

I felt pretty fabulous when I turned fifty, not fantastically over-the-moon fabulous—but pretty fabulous, an eight, on a scale of one to ten, a solid eight. I had a life that was meaningful, a career that was gratifying, a husband who loved me unconditionally, and friends who I loved and treasured. A beautiful home, a great apartment, and I had an abundance of hope and determination.

Fifty-one started out a bit iffy, a bit shaky. I had all the above, except my hope and determination began to dwindle. It was as if I woke up one morning, having taken a handful of bitter and resentful pills the night before. Any form of intimacy felt like an invasion. I would tell my husband "no" on a daily, consistent basis. This could be categorized as the *"through richer, through poorer, through sickness, through health, through anger, through stay away from me or* I'LL STAB YOU" part of our vows. I bought two brand-new Mac computers (one laptop, one desktop) thinking that this would jumpstart my writing career.

That's somewhat equivalent to buying a brand-new Viking range thinking you'll enjoy cooking more, even though you've never liked cooking in the first place.

Fifty-two was slightly under horrific. The flicker of hope and determination I had the year before had vanished, not to mention a career that not only went south but went south and was obliterated by a hurricane. And on top of that, I no longer had a waistline. I COULD NOT ZIP UP ONE PAIR OF PANTS OR JEANS. NOT ONE PAIR. The zipper would stop about a quarter inch above my pubic bone. Refusing to glide up any further. To not embarrass myself, I did not lie down on the floor, holding in both my stomach and my breath simultaneously while trying to zip. You can only do that when you're sixteen and each leg is the width of a baseball bat. I wore the same pair of sweatpants almost daily. Sweatpants, hooded T-shirts, or hooded sweatshirts, depending on the weather. I felt and looked like the *Unawriter.* I always assumed that I would be a fashion statement when I hit midlife. I don't know why I assumed this, other than my deep love for clothes, shoes, and mix 'n' matching—not to mention accessorizing. I love accessorizing. But more than wearing the jewelry, I love buying the jewelry. I have more necklaces that I "had to have" than I could ever wear in this or any lifetime. A stand-back-or I'll-kill-you purchase. I just assumed that I would be a "black sheath, Mikimoto opera-length pearls" type of woman when I hit fifty. I did not expect to be the older version of my much younger hippie self, a *Glamour* DON'T" if ever there was one.

Fifty-three has been a much-needed relief. I'm feeling a bit more these days, as in: a bit more passionate, a bit more creative, a bit more beautiful, a bit more desirable, and a bit more generous, and much, much less bitter and angry.

AND THIS IS MUCH MORE OF A RELIEF FOR MY HUSBAND THAN FOR ME.

TWENTY-SIX

HOW *HIS* GARDEN GR☉WS

HERE'S THE DEAL, A WEEKLY OCCURRENCE IN THE SPRING AND SUMMER MONTHS.

I knock on the garden window, I get my husband's attention, mouthing the words: *"Hey, I'm horny."* He nods and smiles. I nod and smile. He motions to his dirty garden clothes, as if to say, *"Gimme five minutes, I'll be right in."* I respond with a hearty thumbs-up. He hurries, planting the lettuce and arugula seeds at record speed. Five minutes comes and goes. He quickly plants another group of seedlings. Then waters the freshly planted vegetables in the freshly composted soil. I can smell the manure from inside the house. He's such a proud gardener. He surveys his entire plot. All the beautiful stone beds that he made from rock and stone from our property. Raised beds. He takes another moment, and pees. He likes to pee outside. It's a guy thing. He pees, he smiles, he's a proud man. This is his garden. It was a tiny little garden just a few years earlier; now it's a field of gorgeous flowers, and vegetables. Our friend refers to it as the Matisse of gardens. A couple of minutes later, maybe five, six minutes later, I can hear the basement door open and shut. I can hear his footsteps bounding up the stairs two at a time. I can hear him rustling through the drawer in his night table. I can hear the clothes being tossed onto the floor. I can hear him getting comfy in bed, *"All ready."*

I AM NO LONGER HORNY. I tell him it was a window. Wrong. It wasn't a window, it was a small, little, tiny glass pane, he says. I can tell he's very disappointed. I can also tell that he took a Cialis, which from all the TV ads I've seen could possibly last a good thirty-six to forty-eight hours, unless you are into horseback riding, which could diminish the effect by almost thirty hours.

He gets dressed, goes back out, and works his garden with more passion and vigor and energy.

His garden is tended to SO beautifully these days.

Ken's gorgeous garden.

TWENTY-SEVEN

THE CAT
IN THE BOX

WISHES HAS NOT SLEPT WITH ME FOR THREE NIGHTS.
I say me, and not us, because truth be told, he really is *my* cat.
He loves Ken, he does, but he *loooves* me more. For almost his
entire cat life he has slept right next to me, on my side of the
bed. He's not an overly affectionate cat, but most definitely he
is a loyal "down to the bone" cat. So loyal in fact, that when I
bound out of bed at 3:00 AM, he bounds along with me. Curls
up on my couch, in my room, while I sit at my computer. And
when I go back to bed, he is right behind.

For the last three nights, he hasn't slept with me, followed me,

or curled up on the couch in my room while I have feverishly

googled: Feline Kidney Failure.

We got him right before we got married. For the record, I was not a cat person. The only reason we got a cat was that when you're living in the woods (even if only on weekends) the chances of mice throwing a late-night party in your kitchen with music and a DJ are pretty much a definite. I deferred to Ken on this, since I am a city girl and have the apartment exterminator on speed dial. Ken said we should get a cat. Me being me, I decided to argue this point—what about calling an exterminator, surely there are many capable exterminators in a rural area. He reminded me that he is an ORGANIC GARDENER and doesn't want any CRAP sprayed anywhere near the garden or the house for that matter, *otherwise the fruits and vegetables and . . . flowers and . . . greens will be poisoned.*

"And . . . and . . . ?" I said, coaxing him along, hoping for a much more "reasonable" answer than the poison excuse.

He looked at me, his mouth wide open, I looked at him, my mouth wide open, and I believe at that moment we were both thinking the exact same thought: "And I'm marrying this person, why?"

Okay. A cat.

I told Ken that I wanted to choose the cat. He called a friend who said he knew someone who was giving away kittens. The kittens were living in a trailer, tucked in the woods, in an isolated area. There were twelve kittens crying and screaming and yelping and freaking the fuck out when I got there. I saw this little tiny gray and white cat. *He looked at me, I looked at him. A connection.* Sort of like what happens in a neighborhood bar late at night after you've had four, five drinks. *Maybe this'll be the one, the girl thinks.* MAYBE I'LL GET LAID, THE GUY THINKS. But trust me, neither thinks they're going to end up in a cat carrier in the back of a car.

I chose the little gray and white cat. The woman, whose name I cannot recall, who also lived in the trailer, told me she named him Aloysius. I thought, how do you have the time to name each cat, and on top of that give one a name that's impossible to pronounce or spell? But I said thank you and left.

As I drove back to the house, this cat with the impossible name cried the entire time.

Ken and I named him Wishes. We were going to name him Al, but Al seemed a little too urban.

I fell madly in love with him, and I have prayed every night that his biological mother doesn't come back for him.

He has slept next to me every night (well, almost every night) for fifteen and a half years.

But now, he's very sick. Deathly sick. We keep him alive with fluids and pills, and a great vet, Dr. Kaplan, helps us keep him alive. He's become weak and sad and has lost weight, and his eyes no longer sparkle and his coat is dull, and we try our best to nurture and love him. Ken and Wishes have bonded on a deep, guy level.

Wishes is skin and bones, and I know, I know that keeping him alive is cruel and inhumane. He is not eating or drinking water. My friend Karen comes with me to the vet, not Dr. Kaplan, because Dr. Kaplan is in New York City and I just can't drive that far, not with my heart breaking. We go to a local vet in Pennsylvania, Karen's vet. Karen is so kind and loving and holds my hand. The vet weighs him. He is down to five pounds. I ask to have a few moments alone with him.

I ask Wishes what he wants me to do. He lays his head down on the metal table. And he closes his eyes. He is tired. He is old and tired and, oh, so very ill. I make a decision.

I can't breathe or catch my breath or see anything because I am crying so hard that everything is FOGGY and DULL. I need to call Ken. I tell Ken that Wishes died, and he cries. The vet asks about cremation. No, I say, we'll bury him in our back yard. He puts Wishes's remains in a small white cardboard-box coffin (which looks just like a KFC box by the way), and I ask the vet to please put Wishes on the back seat of my car.

As it happens, we've had one ice storm after another in Pennsylvania. Even I know that there is no way that Ken can dig a hole-slash-grave while our entire property looks like Dr.

Zhivago's ice palace. We need to find a cold, dry transitional place until we can bury him. Since we aren't going to purchase a freezer at Best Buy, the next best obvious choice is our garaged Miata. We place the box in the trunk, cover the box with a blanket, and decide it's best to not tell any of our friends. However, a few nights later, at a dinner at our house,

we spill the beans. Some laugh. Some cover their mouths. Some never call us again. But every single one of them looks on curiously as they pass the garage. Some even want to touch the trunk.

In the middle of the night, I go out to the garage. I imagine Wishes in the box, in the trunk, and I want more than anything to get a pickax and dig a hole and bury . . . THE MIATA.

After we buried Wishes some time later, I called my mom. I finally told her that Wishes had died. That we had to put him down, that he was very sick and very old and very tired.

"Oh, my god," she gasped, then asked:

"How long were you married?"

My cat. My mother. I have lost them both.

TWENTY-EIGHT

A BURNING QUESTION

I wake up in the middle of the night.

I am drenched.

Every inch.

Head to toe. A hot flash has enveloped me.

Soaked.

I strip down naked, a cold compress on my neck.

I put on a clean, fresh oversized T-shirt.

I don't know exactly when, but I fall back to sleep.

I weigh myself first thing in the morning. I have gained two pounds (okay, maybe not two pounds, but I have definitely retained water weight and *feel* two pounds heavier than when I went to bed).

My editor, Krista, tells me via email that I should get rid of the scale. Throw it away. Bad scale. I do this obediently.

Ken asks me where the scale is—because Ken loves weighing himself—and I tell him that I put it down in the basement where all the rest of the shit is.

With that, he decides to guess his weight.
Oh, same as yesterday.

TWENTY-NINE

ROUND AND ROUND WE GO

LOS ANGELES 2008.

We are here for four days on business—my husband's business. I tag along. I get to see many friends. I get to shop on Montana Avenue. I get to see all the friendly salespeople at Barneys NY/LA, who welcome me with open arms, free samples, and invitations to chip-and-dip parties.

IT IS 3:00 AM, AND I AM WIDE AWAKE.

My husband is sleeping.

I have now tossed and turned for what feels like an entire year.

I can't seem to get any Internet service. I go downstairs to

the business center on the second floor. I am wearing an

oversized T-shirt and flannel pajama bottoms. I am bloated.
I am taking some Chinese herbal concoction, which I bought
from a hyphenate: a Chinese herbalist-slash-artist on Abbott-
Kinney Boulevard—he tells me it's for the bloating, water
retention, and could be, maybe, a possible thyroid imbalance. I
pay a small fortune for these herbs. I am not at all losing any of
the bloat. I am not peeing eight to ten times a day as promised.
I am, however, drinking "gallons" of water suggested. Suffice
it to say, I look four months pregnant. There is a rock 'n' roll
party happening on the first floor.

I am stunned that a young, gorgeous woman is sitting at
the computer. I ask her how long she'll be. She says *oh, like,
twenty-five, thirty, forty, forty-five minutes.* I motion to the
little printed-out sign above the computer: PLEASE KEEP
COMPUTER USE TO FIFTEEN MINUTES MAXIMUM. I ask
her how long she's been on the computer. A fair question. She
looks at me, with her dewy skin and perfectly coiffed hair,
and blue mascara-ed eyelashes and Jimmy Choo's clicking
and tapping to the beat of the music that's pouring up from
the first floor. *She gives me the kind of look that is meant to
intimidate me.*

I am intimidated.

After all, I am the one wearing pajama bottoms.

"LISTEN," I say, my hands firmly planted on my flannel pajama hips, trying to squeeze away the bloat while being tough and seeking sympathy at the same time, "I AM A WOMAN IN MENOPAUSE."

"Wow. You don't look THAT old."

I warm toward her.
"Really? How old do you think I look?"
 Fishing.

A once-over.

"Oh, I don't know, uh, maybe like, uh, like forty- . . . three, forty-four. Give or take."

"Give or take, what, a year . . . three years . . . ten years?" I continue on my fishing expedition.

"Forty-three. You look maybe, like, definitely forty-three."

I want this woman to be my friend. I think of something to say, an icebreaker. As she types away on the computer keyboard, I ask if she's on Google.

She nods. And then the best part, she says: *"An old boyfriend. What a fucking loser."*

We bond.

She goes down one flight to her rock 'n' roll party; I go up four floors to my room.

I crawl into bed. I watch as my sweet husband sleeps—eye mask, earplugs, and lip drool—and can't help but think:

Could I be any luckier?

THIRTY

M⊘THERLESS CHILD
Bea—Part 4

I AM VISITING MY MOTHER FOR THE THIRD TIME IN SEVEN MONTHS. She has moved up the rung rapidly from *independent living* to *assisted living.* I am visiting for an entire week. Suffice it to say, this is an all-inclusive package: a seven-day, six-night, all the abuse you can take, plus airfare. This particular package has no discounts or refunds.

The first "day" is uneventful.

It is the middle of the night. I, of course, can't sleep. I am reading *Always Maintain a Joyful Mind.* My mother comes into the guest room. She stands at the foot of the bed. She wants me to clean up the mess "in there." "In there" is her bedroom.

Her room smells like a litter box. This is not the mother I know.

And yet, at the same time it is the exact same mother I know. Does that make sense? It shocks me how much she has deteriorated in such a relatively short period of time. It shocks me, it saddens me, and, truth be told, it embarrasses me deeply. She no longer bathes daily (or weekly for that matter), she uses a Sharpie marker in lieu of an eyebrow pencil, and her clothes are stained and dirty. It *deeply and painfully* embarrasses me. Now I know how she felt when I was a teenager, going through my "I'm dropping out of high school to go live on a commune" rebellious stage.

As I rip off the wet sheets, replacing them with clean sheets, she stands naked, rummaging through her closet. Searching, looking desperately for a housecoat, "her favorite housecoat." I ask her what it looks like—on the off chance that maybe I can help her find it. *"Help me find it?"* she says in a tone that is both nasty and condescending and brings me right back to my childhood.

I AM NOW A LITTLE GIRL SHOPPING WITH HER MOTHER.

Abraham and Straus. Or, as we *Long Island* girls called it, A&S. My mother was a shopper. She was, on some days, a ferocious warrior shopper. Grabbing, taking, hoarding, seizing every single piece of clothing she could manage to hold, embrace in her two arms. This image could be likened to cradling a baby, although my mother would never be caught cradling a baby or any child for that matter, especially in her arms.

There we were in A&S, a FEEDING FRENZY of sweater sets and slacks and Pucci shifts and bathing-suit cover-ups and more shifts and shoes and boots on sale. I am tugging, grabbing at her ribbed sweater, because she doesn't have a free hand for me to hold as we wind our way toward the dressing room, where we will now spend a good portion of the afternoon as my mother tries on every piece of clothing all while a cigarette dangles from her lips. As I think of this now, I am in awe that none of these department stores burned to the ground while women twirled, catching every angle in the triptych mirror. Perhaps *this* is the miracle of shopping.

My mother always went to the last dressing room in the back. I have no idea why she did that, and even after many years of Buddhist practice, and some dabbling with therapy, I never touched on that particular issue. Although, come to think of it: Being in the very back, tucked away in the corner, out of sight . . . therein probably lies the answer to all my neuroses and deep fears.

I sit on a chair. I offer an opinion only if asked. And mostly, I wasn't *asked* asked—I was *looked-at* asked; the upturn of an eyebrow, or a wink, or a shrug, as in, *"Whatdya think?"* And my opinion was pretty much the same:

"You look so pretty, Mommy."

My mother did not want me to be witty, smart, sassy, or big.

She wanted me to be small, invisible. She wanted me to tug,

grab, and pull at her when she walked in front of me. AND

I JUST WANTED TO BE NEAR HER. I loved watching her

try on clothes: checking every angle, holding in her belly, looking at her rear, hands on hips, leaning into the mirror, pulling back from the mirror, taking in her profile. Fluffing up her hair. Sucking in her cheekbones. Puckering her lips. It was a performance. And then, when all was tried on, and then *tried on again* for good measure, she would read all the labels. Wash. Dry-clean. Cotton. Silk. Linen. Wool. Polyester. Cashmere. And then once she made her final decision, she would fold each and every piece of clothing that she decided to buy, so that every single crease was perfectly matched.

As she undressed, she would place her cigarette in the ashtray. All of a sudden there it was. Her vagina. Of course I had seen it before: in the shower, in the bathtub, when she got dressed to go out with my dad. I saw her vagina often, but in a changing room? *This* was not allowed. This was a rule, a law. Forbidden. There were signs saying that you had to wear *undergarments* when you tried on clothing. Especially bathing suits. My mother was breaking the dressing room law, and I was a witness.

"Mommy?"

"YES, AMY."

"Mommy, you're not wearing panties."

She bends down—her naked body crouching in front of me, and in a hushed voice, "YOU KNOW MOMMY DOESN'T LIKE WEARING PANTIES SOMETIMES."

I nod.

"LET'S MAKE THIS OUR SECRET. OKAY?"

I nod.

"YOU KNOW WHAT HAPPENS TO LITTLE GIRLS WHO KEEP THEIR MOMMIES' SECRETS?"

"Uh-uh. What?"

"THEY GET PRESENTS."

I smile.

And then the zinger—the nasty, condescending, biting zinger: "AND DO YOU KNOW WHAT HAPPENS TO LITTLE GIRLS WHO DON'T KEEP THEIR MOMMIES' SECRETS?"

No, I shake my head, no.

She takes a drag. Exhales.
And with great, deliberate precision:
"GOD. WILL. PUNISH. THEM."

She stands up.

I am face to face with her vagina.

Maybe it was the tone she used when she said, "God. Will. Punish. Them." Or maybe it was the way she wouldn't let me hold her hand after we left the dressing room. Maybe it was the silence in the car ride home, or the closing—slamming—of her bedroom door when we got home. Or maybe, just maybe, it was the way she said, *"Help me find it?"* But this is where the little girl in the dressing room and the grown-up woman changing her mother's sheets become one, blend together, stand side by side.

My mother finds her favorite housecoat. It is hanging behind her bedroom door on a hook. She is back in bed. The sheets are clean. I shut the lights. She says thank you. I say you're welcome, sleep tight.

Then this is what my mother says to me as I am closing her door:

"I never wanted anyone to love you. I wanted everyone to love me."

This is where the little girl and the grown-up woman part ways.

The grown-up Amy crawls into bed with her mother and holds her. She tells her mother that she doesn't need her to love her in the way that she desperately needed her to when she was a little girl. She tells her mother that she has so much love in her life, a gracious plenty.

Her mother seems extraordinarily relieved by this. A burden lifted. Then she asks Amy, "Do you love me?" Amy says, "Yes."

Her mother falls asleep—in her arms—like a baby.

THIRTY- ONE

THE NEW YAWKER

Sometimes in the middle of the night, when all is quiet, and I believe that anything is possible, I envision, in my wild imagination, that I'm a cartoonist for THE NEW YORKER magazine.

I would love to be like a Gahan Wilson type of cartoonist. But I'm not.

(For those who are not familiar with Gahan Wilson's cartoons, they're black-and-white line sketchy, very New York neurotic.)

surgeons

plastic...or paper?

THIRTY-TWO

I WALK THE FOG LINE

This is one of those "you had to be there" moments.

IT IS 2:30 IN THE MORNING. We are driving from our apartment in New York City to our home in Pennsylvania. This is not something I enjoy doing at all. I am cranky and bitter and I hope that Ken will think I am too unstable to be in the car with him. No such luck. He's got my number. This is something Ken loves to do. Under the "LOVES TO DO" category, I always have a long list or, at the very least, a fairly long list. Mine usually includes visiting Paris, getting facials, four- and/or five-star hotels, room service, thumbing through catalogues in the middle of the night, watching *Mad Men,* and going to MoMA. Ken has two things on his "LOVES TO DO" list. The first is gardening; the second is the 90-minute drive home to Pennsylvania at any ungodly hour. I prefer the gardening.

This is merely a glimpse into our private, and personal, conversation.

(A is Amy, K is Ken.)

A: Please drive slower, hon.

K: I am driving slower, babe.

A: Slower than what, moo-moo?

K: Slower than the last time you asked me, sweetie.

A: **Okay** *(accompanied by a deep, loud, obnoxious sigh),* **thanks.**

K: Uh, huh.

(Silence for about ten minutes, then)

A: Please drive slower, Ken.

K: I am driving slower, Amy.

A: Slower. Than. What?

K: THAN. THE. LAST. TIME. YOU. ASKED. ME.

A: I DOUBT THAT.

(Silence again. Another ten minutes, then)

A: SLOW DOWN.

K: FUCK YOU.

A: *NO, NO, NO FUCK YOU, KEN. FUCK YOU!!!!!!!!!*

K: *Okay. That's it. Get outta the car, I'm pulling over and I want you outta the fucking car. I've had enough of this shit.*

A: *Yeah. Right.* ASSHOLE.

K: *(Mimicking me) Yeah. Right.*
(Ken does not say *asshole*. He hates that word. He finds it nasty and mean-spirited, and since he is a much better human being than I am, he refrains from tossing it back.)

(A beat.)

A: PLEASE. DRIVE. SLOWER.

K: YOU DRIVE.

A: I DON'T WANNA DRIVE. IF I WANTED TO DRIVE, I'D BE DRIVING.

K: You are driving.

We can no longer look at each other. I have wedged myself between the seat and the passenger door. My body language says: tense, pissed, don't touch me. Ken stares out the windshield, he's mumbling under his breath, I can swear I hear him saying cocksucker, motherfucker but decide to ignore his childish behavior. However, I am betting that *we are both* planning nasty divorce proceedings.

YOU GET THE DRIFT.

THIRTY-THREE

BABY BOOMER-RANG

I TELL KEN THAT I AM SUFFERING FROM VAGINAL DRYNESS. He looks at me as if I am blaming him for this. His back shoots straight up, his head tilts, and his mouth pinches. He tells me that it was the way I said it—the tone in my voice—that made him feel as if I was pointing the proverbial finger at him. I tell him it's the way he's interpreting the way I'm saying it that puts him on the defensive. This is one of those no-win situations.

I tell him just because he needs to have sex on a much more regular basis than I do is absolutely no reason for him to think for one second that my pain and discomfort, along with my chronic atrophic vaginitis, is in any way, shape, or form because of his desperate need to prove that he's still virile. He tells me to blow myself. I TELL HIM I'M TOO DRY.

Possibly there's a solution. I am sitting at my computer googling *vaginal dryness,* and I am delighted that there are over one million sites dedicated to this.

Here is a partial list:

Yesyesyes.org

Amazingsolutions.com

Ceebai.com

Sylkonline.com

Seniorhealth.com

Vaginaldiscomfort.com

And my very favorite:

POWER-SURGE.COM

Each site dedicates a good solid paragraph on how no one talks about painful intercourse. I beg to differ. I'm talking about it every single day to anyone and everyone who will listen. The burning, the itching, the irritation, and, in my particular case, the lovely add-on of an arthritic neck, which makes lying down unbearable. I used to be spontaneous and sexy—a high-heel vixen, okay, maybe not a high-heel vixen, but a good one- to two-inch princess heel always gave me a boost—now I need pillows and props and two-pound weights around my ankles to keep me from flailing. On VAGINALDISCOMFORT.COM they claim that this is all part of the maturing process, on fuckingtoomuch.com they believe it's all a part of being tremendously promiscuous when we were younger, and on YESYESYES.COM they are huge advocates of saying no-no-no to dryness with K-Y Jelly and some foam thing that actually lines the vaginal wall with some kind of gooey substance, all while letting you maintain a good healthy attitude. None of them, however, recommends a seven-day, seven-night intercourse regimen; you must become a Christian to get onto that site.

I WRITE MY DOCTOR AN EMAIL IN THE MIDDLE OF NIGHT. In the subject line, I write in caps: PERSONAL. I try to be as easygoing and humorous as possible, which I know is only covering up my deep humiliation and masking my real true feelings: STAY AWAY. I'M JUST NOT IN THE MOOD. It's a simple, cute, funny email. I hit the send button and go about my business.

Color me surprised when he responds within ten minutes. At first I think this is so cool and groovy: My doctor—my personal physician, not some faceless *Web*MD tech person who is making believe he's a doctor—is online at 3:17 in the morning, and as I'm about to respond to his email, I think,

wait a sec, I am actually having what feels like an IM conversation with my doctor in the middle of the night, asking him about vaginal suppositories and creams so I can have sex—comfortable, happy sex—with my husband.

Oh, it feels creepy.

I quickly get off-line.

And, for good measure, to cleanse and rid myself,

I shut down my computer.

THIRTY-FOUR

JUST SAY NO

Okay, come on, how many of us say yes when we really, truly, deeply want to say no? Raise your hands. I, for one, lie in bed thinking about all the things I should say no to that I say yes to on a daily basis. This could even be filed as such: MARRIAGE, FRIENDSHIP, FAMILY, WORK–SLASH–BUSINESS LIFE, and ACQUAINTANCES. Everything from *"Sure I can whip up pumpkin pancakes with fresh fruit compote"* to *"Of course I can go shopping with you right now and discard my own life"* to *"Of course I can loan you money—I am, after all, an ATM."*

IT'S AN ADDICTION. I think of starting a twelve-step program: *Yes Anonymous.* I am sure I can find many, many people to join this group. This is a conversation I have had with many friends—both women and men—who suffer from the very same compulsion, although my friend Claire says it's not a compulsion, it's pathological and could even be hereditary. I want to tell her, *"No, you're wrong, it's not pathological, it's an addiction, and one cannot pass on the yes gene, although one can learn from a parent to be extremely passive, along with having the inability to make a commitment,"*

but of course, I say, yes, you're right, it's pathological.

I have read numerous books and articles on this topic, ranging from a weekly column to a monthly Q&A.

THIS HAS BECOME A HOT-BUTTON TOPIC. It seems that along with restless leg syndrome, the inability to say no is one popular cyber, not to mention secular, discussion. This is a curiosity for me, something that plagues me often. I wonder, sometimes out loud, how all of these maladies were dealt with years ago. I'm sure people had restless leg syndrome twenty-five years ago, and I'm absolutely positive that folks said yes when they meant no—particularly women—starting, oh, I don't know, a guess, at the beginning of time. Did it all just go under the category of "SENILE" or "INSANE"? Did folks get lobotomies and shock therapy for this kind of stuff? Or is it that it went under the heading of "PATHOLOGICAL LYING." Now there are books and workshops and medication and weekend retreats and yoga poses to deal with these issues. Back then, you were committed and left to rot. And to think there are some people out there who don't believe in evolution.

In any event, as usual, I digress. Here is a list of my favorite books and/or articles on the subject of manifesting a good, solid no.

The Dis-ease To Please

The Power of No

A Happy No Is a Happy Family

The Power of Yes

The Torment of Withholding

The Real You, the Fake You

The Bigger the No, the Larger the Yes

Fuck You, Fuck Me, Fuck No!

The Weak Say Yes, the Strong Say No, and the Enlightened Human Being Says: Maybe!

MY HUSBAND WOULD LIKE FOR ME TO MENTION AS AN ASIDE THAT I SAY NO TO HIM WITHOUT ANY PROBLEM.

THIRTY-FIVE

iM©VIE POSTERS

Sometimes, when I can't sleep and I'm bored, I humor myself by taking an all-male buddy movie, or one of those horribly violent, vulgar, disgusting masochistic movies, and I add my very own feminine/feminist spin.

Now, imagine the poster: sepia tone, turn of the century. A woman standing in a field, in the background an oil rig—she looks completely and utterly at wits' end. Her arms and clenched fists stretch upward toward the heavens. In the very corner of the poster, her family, huddling together, clearly frightened of her.

THERE WILL BE *NO* BLOOD

Starring Daniel Day-Lewis as a menopausal woman who no longer gets her period.

An epic love story:

Girl finds Self.

THIRTY-SIX

THE
NAKED
CITY

MANY YEARS AGO when I was working the Hollywood beat as a screenwriter I was good friends with a guy (who shall remain nameless) who was (and still is) a relatively big-shot studio executive. We were "good friends," not the "friends with benefits" kind of friends—you know, the sexual party favors and the occasional sleeping together—just good, old *plain* friends.

He lived in a McMansion on top of Mulholland Drive. *Now I want to preface this by saying that I had been TO his house many times, but I had never been INSIDE his house.* I was in L.A. on business and we were going out to dinner. Instead of meeting at the restaurant, I told him I'd pick him up. I got to his house and I had to pee really, really badly. I buzzed the intercom asking him to let me in, he buzzed back saying he would be right out, I said, "NO, NO, NO . . . I have to pee." He said,

"NO, NO, NO . . . I'll be right out." *"YOU HAVE TO LET ME IN!" I demanded. "YOU HAVE TO HOLD IT!" He was emphatic. I yanked out a very big chit from the little deck: If he didn't let me in, I'd pee in his Porsche. Dead silence.*

He had a very inappropriate relationship with his Porsche. I say this with both a straight face and much actual proof—*if he COULDA had children with his Porsche, he WOULDA.* With great reluctance, he let me in. When I walked into his home, there was absolutely not one piece of furniture with the exception of a mattress on the floor, a multiline phone right next to the mattress, and, tucked into the corner of this massive room, a TV set and VCR. HIS HOUSE, JUST LIKE MOTHER HUBBARD'S CUPBOARD, WAS COMPLETELY FUCKING BARE.

I never could look at him quite the same after that.

THE POINT IS—IT'S WHAT'S BEHIND THE DOOR THAT HOLDS ALL THE TRUTH.

Which brings me to my closet.

My closet has a collection of clothing that dates back to when I was a size 2. I would say that a good 65 percent of the clothing in my closet not only doesn't fit me but also, as an aside, no longer looks good on a hanger.

On one of those *"Should I read another book?"* kind of middle of the nights, I have what appears to be an epiphany: *Aha,* I think, *it's the perfect time to clean out the closet.* It gives me both something to do and an opportunity to reflect on a life well lived. Or perhaps, more appropriately, a life well worn. As I rummage through my closet, I am imagining each piece of clothing—*which, after a good hour or so, I am feverishly tossing into a huge, black hefty garbage bag that I will drop off at the local Salvation Army anonymously*—having their very own personal episode on the History Channel. Each piece of clothing has a "tell-all," if you will.

There are eight million stories in my closet.

THE BLACK SPANDEX MINIDRESS:
a dark tale of desperation, and unrequited love.
Love me, love me, *LOVE me*! Please, please, *PLEASE*!

THE PADDED SHOULDER "TO MIDTHIGH" SWEATER:
a story of shame, guilt, and an illegal amount of alcohol not to mention a staircase, a broken heel, and a faceless/nameless man and a very long cab ride to the Upper West Side.

THE LONG, GRAY DOUBLE-BREASTED—
WITH BELT—NORMA KAMALI TRENCH COAT:
the story of a nightclub-slash-bar, a very sad unfortunate break-up, and the middle-of-the-night sobbing phone call that went along with it.

THE SIZE 4 CALVIN KLEIN JEANS:
Does this one even need a story?

THE SIZE SMALL DIANE VON FURSTENBERG WRAP-DRESS:
the story of a particularly bad date, projectile vomiting, and a
spritz of eau *de infidelity.*

THE HIGH-WAISTED BALLOON
PANTS AND MATCHING VEST:
the story of a screenwriting interview gone terribly awry.

WHAT APPEARS TO BE A WIDE BLACK LEATHER BELT
BUT TURNS OUT TO BE A MINISKIRT:
This doesn't have a story, because there doesn't seem
to be a body that went along with it.

A LONG, ANKLE-LENGTH,
SHAPELESS FLORAL-PRINT SCHMATA:
This could be one of two stories—the story of playing hide-
and-seek with your very own body *("Oh, look, I found my leg")*
or an attempt to be Amish.

A GIORGIO ARMANI BLACK AND
WHITE TWEED (PANT) SUIT, SIZE 4:
the story of a struggling, poor writer trying to be a hyphenate:
"Writer-slash-hey-notice-me-I'm-a-cool-chick-with-taste-not-
to-mention-a-massive-balance-on-my-Visa-card."

THE SKIN-TIGHT, APRICOT BETSEY JOHNSON
CRUSHED-VELVET ONE-PIECE JUMPSUIT SIZE S(MALL):
the story of a wanna-be rock 'n' roll star who settles for being a
groupie with a local band that doesn't play anywhere and has
no fan base.

THE OLD SOFT THREADBARE FLANNEL SHIRT:
the story of a piece of clothing that never, ever goes out
of style.

AND . . .

THE LONG, SEXY, BACKLESS
OFF-WHITE WEDDING GOWN SIZE 4:
the story of a relationship with a happy ending. Amy and Ken.

This one stays in the closet.

THIRTY-SEVEN

K&THY

Kathy died in her sleep.

SHE WAS MY BEST FRIEND.

As in: the one who encouraged me to be a writer, to marry

Ken, to stop being so self-indulgent, to take risks, to try

harder, to move on, to be kinder to myself, to love myself more

and others just a bit less, to create, to share, to forgive, to not

just practice Buddhism but to be a Buddha, to visit my mother,

to stand up to my brother, to demand justice, to denounce

self-hatred, to find a good shopping bargain, to spend less

money on shoes and more time on Ken, to write from my soul
and to stop caring what others think.

THE KIND OF BEST FRIEND WHO TELLS YOU WHEN
YOU'RE ABSOLUTELY FULL OF SHIT, who holds you when
the pain of a break-up seems just so unbearable that you don't
believe for one second that this suffering will ever go away,
and who tells you as you are sobbing, heaving, snot nose and
all, into her favorite sweater: *"Fuck him, he'll die a lonely, sad,*
pathetic man who never deserved you in the first place."

Yes, that kind of best friend.

Kathy had breast cancer, then it went into remission, then a
couple of years later it spread throughout her body like wild
fire—her breasts, her lungs, her bones. *We had known each*
other for close to thirty-five years. After she married Michael,
she moved to Maryland, and we lost touch for a few years,
then found each other again, and for a good solid ten years
we spoke twice a week, saw each other five, six times a year,
and then the final two years of her life, we spoke every single
day. She went on a very strict cleansing, juicing diet. Along
with Michael, all her friends (and she had plenty) took turns
taking care of her. But the thing about Kathy that to this day
still amazes me—HER UNYIELDING GENEROSITY. She had
always wanted me to meet Tina, Tina Smith, but for various
reasons, we had never met face to face. She had known all
about me, I had known all about her. Kathy loved sharing
friends. She loved sharing, period. But she was quite adamant
that Tina and I meet. We did. Kathy introduced us to each

other by saying, *"I love you both; please, love each other."* I can now say with great pleasure that Tina is one of my dearest and closest friends. Tina is the kind of friend you can tell anything to and she will undoubtedly have the best answer because of her wisdom and, guess what, not only lead you to the right place, but when you get there, Tina will be the one ready to hold your hand and walk you through the entire obstacle course because she has been there first. Tina is a true blue friend. A gift from Kathy.

The last time I saw Kathy she couldn't walk very well. She was frail and thin but absolutely gorgeous. Her spirit was untainted by the disease.

We were curled up on her couch, and I asked her if she could do anything, anything at all, what would that be. *She said she would want to fly, like really fly, like spread her arms and just . . . fly.* I THOUGHT SHE WAS GOING TO SAY, "I WOULD BE HEALTHY." But that wasn't who Kathy was. Kathy had no regrets. She wasn't looking at the cancer as "if only," she was seeing it as a piece within a big life. She lived. She loved. She struggled. She was victorious. She had great sadness. She had great joy. She had disappointments. She had great victories. She had Michael. She loved him madly. He loved her more. And oh by the way she had cancer.

A couple of nights later, back at home, I dreamt that Kathy was standing on the edge of a cliff, and then . . . she flew. I watched her fly. I bolted up knowing that Kathy had just died.

It was the middle of the night.

THE PHONE RANG.

It was Michael.

He woke up (having fallen asleep in a chair), sensing a huge, deep, sudden emptiness, he went to their bedroom, and there was Kathy, completely and utterly at peace.

I have to say that I absolutely loved that I was able to watch her fly, even though it meant away from me.

THIRTY-EIGHT

9½ YEARS
a.k.a. the 3:47 AM Blues

I am trying to be less self-conscious about my body. This is not easy for me. And quite honestly, I personally don't know many women (well, maybe one) who can stand naked in front of a full-length mirror and not gasp out loud at the sight of their newfound peri-, meno-, or postmenopausal body. I really don't know anyone. Even my most diehard feminist friends when standing in front of their mirror are a teeny bit (come on, be honest) mortified that there is no longer a body they recognize or even want to take out to a movie and dinner. There was a time—I was younger, much younger—when my body was pretty fabulous, not unlike Kim Basinger's body in *9½ Weeks*. Okay, that's an outright lie. If I had Kim Basinger's body I would have been a professional ice skater, not a junior-league bowler. But the real kick: I NEVER, EVER EXERCISED. Never. I always skipped gym class. I also skipped every other class, but that's another story, another chapter. My mother told me I was extremely lucky to have such a lovely slim body. She also managed to tell me in the same breath that luck—just like anything—could be taken away from you in a flash. So, I was lucky to have a slim, thin, lovely body but, per my mother, also acutely aware and extremely open-minded to the fact that all this luck would be taken right out from under me at even given moment without forewarning. Let's put it this way: I did not stack all my hard-boiled eggs in one lucky basket. But not to dwell on this, I'll fast-forward.

MY BODY:

I WANT *to be uninhibited.*

I WANT *to embrace my midriff excess.*

I WANT *to love my body; I want to accept this new voluptuality (yes, a made-up word, a combination of voluptuous and sexuality), which just yesterday I called round and fleshy.*

I WANT *to feel sexual and sexy and intimate making love with Ken, rather than being the one on the receiving end. I believe it's called being "generous and pro-active."*

I WANT *to wear a pair of sexy panties and a sexy bra, a pair of fishnet stockings and black patent leather heeled booties, and feel comfortable and at ease and desirable as I walk toward Ken. Flirty. Dangerous. Come hither, baby, and watch me wanting you wanting me. I want to strut my stuff and enjoy—savor—every single moment of it.*

I WANT *to be Lena Olin in* The Unbearable Lightness of Being *for just one night.*

But . . .

I can't help feeling dull and empty. It's sort of like when an engine runs out of gas, it spits and puffs a few times, but basically that's it. It stops running.

So, here's the lowdown as I write this as my husband sleeps next to me, having only a few hours earlier tried to convince me that I was the most beautiful woman he had ever lain eyes on.

WHAT I REALLY, DEEPLY, TRULY WANT IS THIS:

To no longer feel the shame of my own body revolution.
I want to look myself straight head-on in the mirror—full body, head to toe, and be absolutely fucking amazingly completely delighted that there is just so much more of me to love.

Viva Body Revolution!

THIRTY-NINE

THE NO JOY LUCK CLUB

I am going to lose friends because of this chapter.

I am not going to lose them because I have divulged their name(s) but because they will wonder, probably in the middle of the night, if in fact this chapter is about them specifically. I can say now: YES.

Know anyone who ONLY calls when they are: *struggling, challenged, unhappy, unlucky, miserable, desperate, bitter, angry, not getting along with coworkers, without partner, stuck in the subway, sitting in traffic, pissed off at the cab driver,*

their hair is too frizzy, their hair is too straight, too short,
too long, their nails are smudged, mascara is running, legs
are tired, neighbors are nosy, mercury is in retrograde, the
stars are unaligned, the cats aren't pooping, the dog is peeing
everywhere, much too cold, much too hot, can't stand the
heat and hate the kitchen, and what's the big deal anyway
about all this fucking multicolored fall foliage?

And not one, "HOW ARE YOU?"

Ever pick up the phone, and immediately, without a moment's
hesitation, a rant, a rave, and a rage: fuck them, fuck her,
fuck him, fuck the whole family, they all suck, motherfucker,
they're selfish, they're rude, they're self-indulgent, he's nasty,
she's nasty, she's such an asshole, he's such a scumbag, piece of
shit, I have no money, I have no job, I have no friends, nothing
fits me, I missed my plane, I can't get a cab, the bus takes exact
change, my boss is a bitch, my landlord doesn't understand my
financial issues, and I'M GOING TO TELL YOU ONE MORE
TIME THAT HE'S JUST A FUCKING PRICK AND I WANT HIM
OUT OF THE HOUSE ASAP BUT HE'S ABSOLUTELY NOT—
DO YOU HEAR ME—*NOT* CHEATING ON ME.

And you're cradling the phone on your shoulder for a good
two hours listening to the ranting and raving and raging, and
not one *"And hey, what's going on with you?"*

And then the pièce de résistance: when good things are
happening, when they get the job, get the man, the woman,

the transit system seems to be running on time, the sky is blue, the stars are aligned, the flowers are in bloom, the hair is perfectly coiffed, the boss is a peach, the European vacation was jolly perfect, the landlord offered a reprieve, the check came in the mail, and oh my god she thought she was going to get fired, but oh my god she got a fucking raise.

When things are going really swell, when life is good, when no one is a fucking asshole—not a peep. Not a word. Not a call. Not a postcard "wish you were here" or there.

I LIE AWAKE:
Why, oh why, oh why do I want people like this in my life?

AND THEN I WONDER: Should I send a personal note on one of those swell little note cards, or just blast a group email and of course I would blind copy everyone, because I've been reprimanded *(by the very same person-slash-people who don't ask how I am, thank you very much)* more than once for being so very thoughtless and inconsiderate in sending out bulk emails—without blind copying—during the holidays.

NEW GIRLS ON THE BLOCK

"It was an accident, I swear, he fell on the knife."

"Yeah, that's it, he fell on the knife."

Paroled: Bella & Lotus

OH, MY

IT IS ALL-CONSUMING, THIS GUILT. It keeps me up, it keeps me replaying scenes over and over and over until there doesn't seem to be any coherent narrative, let alone make any sense. There is no straight line.

Mothers and daughters, daughters and sons, brothers and sisters, sisters and mothers, mothers and sons . . .

This is the deal: I don't want to visit my mom again. There's a whole bunch of reasons that range from small and trite to deeply painful that run through my mind: everything from not wanting to spend a full day traveling to New Mexico—the whole airport boarding-the-plane fiasco *(I know, I know, small, trite)*—to the sadness I feel when I am there, and how much worse I feel when I leave *(bigger, more understandable, gut-wrenching)*, to the possibility of running into my brother, who I haven't spoken to in almost a full year, with the exception of an occasional email from him, which is always, by the way, in those yelling screaming CAPS *(I know, I know, petty but quite relatable)*.

I grab my computer, propping it up on a pillow so I can be comfy in bed and look up the word "guilt," as I am beginning to think it is not guilt I am feeling. Rather, a knee-jerk reaction that can be mistaken for guilt. This is an opportunity for some clarity. In the *Encarta World English Dictionary* this is the definition of guilt:

1) *An awareness of having done wrong or committed a crime, accompanied by feelings of shame and regret.*

2) *The fact of having committed a crime or done wrong.*

3) *The responsibility for committing a crime or doing wrong.*

4) *The responsibility, as determined by a court or other legal authority, for committing an offense that carries a legal penalty.*

It becomes very clear to me that my family never owned an *Encarta World English Dictionary*. Perhaps it was *Webster's* that defined guilt as relating to home visits, money issues, phone calls, staying out all night, and rebellion, not to mention the whole sibling dynamic/equation.

Okay, we can scratch off guilt, at least by *Encarta's* definition.

Maybe it's just I don't
want to say good-bye again.
Maybe it's just that simple.

But simple is not something I am particularly comfortable with.
Simple doesn't work for me. I prefer emotional chaos, so with
all of this crap swirling around in my mind, I think of my
mother mostly being alone, not all alone *alone,* but she is not
"family and friends" rich and full. It is not—contrary to all
rumors—a Verizon plan.

MY MOTHER AND FATHER, AT ONE TIME, HAD MANY
FRIENDS AND MUCH FAMILY. On any given Friday or
Saturday night, there would be four, six, eight couples at our
house, playing mah-jongg, canasta, gin rummy, pinochle,
drinking, laughing, joking. Over the years friends separated,
husbands died, wives died, a callous remark stuck a little
longer than it should have, a throwaway was more painful
than playful, a jab turned into a stab, a secret was told, a
trust was broken, a memory was forgotten, a house was sold,
a life moved away, and pretty soon where there once were ten
friends, there are now four, and then there is one fewer friend,
and another death and you find yourself alone at the table
with a stranger who you might on some days mistake for your
daughter, the one who mistakes a simple answer for guilt.

My mother had many friends. But then, slowly but surely,
every friend had a flaw, a fault, that insurmountable blemish
that my mother just could not tolerate any longer or silently

as she grew older. She would tell them to their face that they

were ugly or fat or stupid.

As I stare up at the ceiling fan, watching it slowly rotate counterclockwise, I think *this is not how I want to spend the last years, let alone the last months of my life.* I do not want to have a funeral or memorial with only three people attending who not only no longer speak to each other but also have absolutely nothing good to say about each other, let alone me, the dead one. I decide right then and there to forgive all the friends who never ask me how I am, who never say hey how you doing, I will not hit the send button on the email that I composed telling them that due to the recession the woe-is-me hotline is closing down, *because there will come a day when I'm going to need them to fill an entire funeral home,* and speak well of me, and say, boy oh boy, she was such a good friend who listened to all our bullshit over and over and over and over again and never once told us to go fuck ourselves.

Oh, maybe once.

FORTY-TWO

I HEAR NOISES

I hear noises, and I have to say, New York City night noises are way different from deep-in-the-woods/living-in-the-country night noises. I know I'm stating the obvious.

Having weaned myself off New York City gradually, we now live primarily (five out of seven days) in the country, in the woods in Pennsylvania. *I hear noises all the time.* And, yes, I hear them in the middle of the night, but after almost sixteen years, I don't pay *as much* attention. KEY WORDS: AS MUCH. At one time I made Ken buy enough lights and alarms and animal detectors that at any given moment our house would light up like Disney World. This is the truth. Alarms blaring, strobes spinning, and bells ringing, until Ken asked, literally begged me, to please, please, *please* get some help. I did, partially—I spoke with numerous friends who live in the country and they all agreed with me, and sympathized with me, and when I informed Ken that there are many, many women out there who share in my noise issues, he told me I needed professional help, so I went to the only woman I know who has a full-time executive job, and she, too, agreed with me.

What I have learned is this: When you live deep in the woods, there will be noises, and most—not all, but most—are all a part of the big natural wood/landscape.

But this night didn't feel natural. It felt weird and strange, and trust me, this is not going where you think it's going.

I HEAR SCRATCHING. But it seems to be a collection of scratching, and as I walk closer to my living room, tiptoeing toward the French doors, *my heart is pounding, my toes are killing me, and the scratching gets louder and weirder and I flip on the outside light,* and there standing next to each other on my fieldstone patio is a cat and *a big, gigantic, really fucking-ugly-looking rat-type animal*—RIGHT BY THE DOOR. And if this were Halloween, I would swear they were trick *and* treating.

I wake up Ken—actually, I SCREAM, a guttural scream—and I demand he get out of bed now. NOW. I hear the *"Oh, Jesus, what now"* groan, and he begrudgingly gets out of bed, dragging his body to the living room, where he, too, looks out the French door, seeing exactly what I see: a cat and a big, gigantic, really fucking-ugly-looking rat-type animal, and he says:

"THAT'S ONE FUCKING UGLY OPOSSUM," turning to me, as if this would encourage me, "AND A REALLY BIG ONE."

With that, as you can well imagine, I felt so much better.

FORTY-THREE

"GET OUT OF MY FACE" BOOK

IT IS 2:45 IN THE MORNING, AND I AM READING AND ANSWERING EMAILS. Then, the sudden sound effect of incoming emails: Gardens Alive, The Vitamin Shoppe, SkinID, and then one from a newfound friend on Facebook. Actually, not from the new friend herself but from the entire Facebook team alerting me that her birthday is coming up in seven days and would I like to send her a birthday card–slash–greeting.

How sweet.

And as I continue reading, answering other emails, a few more Facebook or, more acurately, *Wallmaster* alerts from folks who are on Facebook, writing on my wall. I'm being informed that they are sending me a message.

Sort of sweet.

And then I get some sort of notification from Plaxo that a few people I know have changed their photos, updated their resumes, moved to a foreign country, are getting divorced, and have changed their last names.

Huh. More than I care to know.

And then I get some crap from Classmates.com, which I have to say is COMPLETE BULLSHIT, because (a) I did not graduate from high school, so I have no classmates, and (b) one of the reasons *(along with the profound desire to* FIND MYSELF—*yes, a cliché, but in the early seventies it was as hip as you can possibly get)* I dropped out of high school was that I had no friends. I was the girl with upper and lower metal braces, curly-fizzy hair, and I was so skinny I looked—as we used to say—like I was from BIAFRA (back then we weren't thinking PC). I felt so inferior to the other girls that I basically kept to myself, except for Saturday League Bowling, where I whipped their asses good. So, Classmates.com is sending me an email informing me that a dozen friends from high school are trying to get in touch with me. *And for $49.99 a year, I can find out what they are now doing. I suspect—and I'm going out on a limb here—not quite as well as I am. Last time I spoke to anyone I grew up with, which was a good fifteen years ago, was to commiserate over the fact our little Long Island town had spawned a* SERIAL KILLER.

THIS NEED TO SOCIALIZE ALL BEGAN IN A LONELY, DARK (MIDDLE OF THE) NIGHT. I was online. Googling, checking emails, trying to figure out if I wanted to buy a pair of Frye boots at Zappos, because they have a great return policy, and I thought, gee wouldn't it be nice to have some friends to "talk" to at 3 or 4 in the morning. I was feeling *"disconnected, alone in the world, a general low-grade malaise,"* and so I registered with Facebook and Plaxo and LinkedIn and all these other social network places.

And then in the morning, after a few hours of sleep, I felt less needy.

And so, because of that one lonely night, I now have more friends and coworkers and acquaintances and high school classmates and old boyfriends than I ever had in "real" life. And of course, just like life, you get a person who thinks they know you, and they write on your wall:

HI, AMY, SO GOOD TO SEE YOU, DIDN'T WE HAVE FUN?

And, you wonder, *fun?* Was I on drugs? Did I really know this person? Did we work together? Or perhaps we did Quaaludes together back when Quaaludes were Rorer 714s? Did we live in the same building?

And so, I respond with a simple answer on her wall *(this is an actual, word-for-word, wall-to-wall correspondence):*

Hi, I'm sorry, I can't place you, how do we know each other?

And then this response on my wall:
REALLY? YOU CAN'T PLACE ME? WE SANG TOGETHER AT
THE VIENNA MUSIC FESTIVAL.

My response on her wall:
I'm sorry. I don't sing. You've mistaken me for someone else.

And her response on my wall:
I know exactly who I sing with, AND I SANG WITH YOU! I sang
with you a month ago. We stood next to each other.

And having just read a piece on the possible behavioral side
effects of Ambien, and all this strange shit that people are
experiencing without any knowledge of what they're doing—
eating full meals plus dessert, driving hundreds of miles,
having sex with strangers—I wonder:

*Huh, did I go to Vienna? Did I sing in the chorus? Did I go to
an airport and have my passport stamped and take off my
shoes at the security checkpoint and sit on a plane in coach
for twelve hours and actually sing with the Vienna Chorus?*

Maybe.

FORTY-FOUR

THE NEWPORT WOMAN

I am longing for a cigarette.

My friend Karen smokes occasionally. She can go months
and months without having one cigarette. She can be at a bar,
surrounded by smokers and drinkers, and have a few cocktails
and shamelessly grub a Newport or Marlboro from a nearby
patron, and then not smoke again for months. I could never do
that. I could not just grub one, smoke it, and leave it at that.

I LOVED,
L.O.V.E.D., SMOKING.

I FELT SEXY AND BAD, AND IT MADE ME COMFORTABLE
KEEPING MY DISTANCE.

A cigarette, I have found, can keep anyone at arm's length.

I don't miss smoking during the day. It's the nights, the late nights when I'm alone, and all is quiet, and I am sitting at my computer and I miss THE CIGARETTE. I miss the lighting of the match, the inhaling, the long exhale, and the cool little smoke rings I made when I was trying to figure out a scene or a sentence. I loved the way it looked in the ashtray, a line of smoke as it made its way up toward the ceiling. Poof. Gone. Sexy-ish.

There was a period of time, perhaps it was *my mourning period*, when I could not write a single word, and I was absolutely convinced that it was connected to my having stopped smoking. NO SMOKING, NO WRITING. Not a cigarette, not a word. I tried googling to see if there was any connection, or if this was my own personal creative withdrawal scenario. How narcissistic is that? Yeah, right, like I am the only person who has given up smoking and simultaneously had a creative block. I found that many people have odd, ritualistic, unique, strange, and even deviant, in some cases, life stories connecting giving up cigarettes to their creativity, hobbies, jobs, husbands, wives, partners, artistic outlets, midlife crises, and sexual habits.

It didn't encourage me, it didn't help me one iota, but it certainly amused me.

Having been a smoker my entire adult life, I gave it up for one reason and one reason only: It just felt completely and utterly right to throw a massive log onto the menopausal fire of my life, sort of like, if you're going through hell, might as well keep on going. Not to mention that Ken hated, H.A.T.E.D., my smoking. Hated the smell, hated how I looked with a cigarette dangling, reminded me daily that those little tiny lip lines could grow deeper and longer and even stretch and expand out toward the cheeks. This didn't scare me one bit.

When I would ask Ken what he wanted for his birthday, our anniversary, Christmas, a few scattered favorite kind of days, he would always say: "I WANT YOU TO STOP SMOK-ING. I WANT YOU TO LIVE LONGER. I WANT YOU TO BE HEALTHY."

Never once saying, I WANT YOU TO BE HAPPY. Because it was all about *living longer,* how selfish is that?

And so, when I bought him sweaters and gloves and garden-ing tools for his birthday, our anniversary, Christmas, and some of those scattered favorite kinds of days, there was al-ways a little teeny twinkle of disappointment in his gorgeous baby blue eyes.

So, you can just imagine how he felt when I announced with great anger and bitterness: I'm giving up smoking. HAPPY NOW?

LET ME SHARE WITH YOU WHAT I MISS ABOUT SMOKING:

I miss the index and middle finger having more power over both the ring and pinky fingers.

I miss the mysterious lighting of the cigarette in a bar, in a restaurant, in a ladies' lounge, as if the spark came out of absolutely nowhere.

I miss feeling like Lillian Hellman sitting at both her type-writer, and at the feet of Dashiell Hammett.

I miss the combination of cold coffee in Styrofoam cups and Newport Lights.

I miss the privacy it gave me.

NOW LET ME TELL YOU WHAT I DON'T MISS:

— *I don't miss the stale smoke smell on all my clothing.*

— *I don't miss the desire to brush my teeth every two hours.*

— *I don't miss the lack of emotional and physical intimacy that it caused between Ken and me.*

— *I don't miss the paying seven bucks a pack—which adds up to over two hundred dollars a month. Uh, holy shit.*

— *I don't miss not being able to breathe or fill up my lungs when I'm walking, stretching, doing yoga, or even getting up out of bed in the middle of the night.*

— *I don't miss having to stand out in the freezing cold,*

bundled and shivering, while trying to actually raise the
cigarette up to my lips because of no smoking signs in restau-
rants, bars, office buildings, airports, hotels, movie theaters,
department stores, post offices, liquor stores, FedEx, Kinko's,
florists, coffee shops, banks, Broadway and/or Off-Broadway
theaters, subways, taxi cabs, and the ladies' rooms.

BUT THERE ARE NIGHTS
like tonight
when I deeply
long
for a Newport.

FORTY-FIVE

THE WHETHER OR NOT CHANNEL

KEN LOVES THE WEATHER CHANNEL. I'm not sure if this is a guy thing, or a Ken thing, or a guy-named-Ken thing, but it is on the one television set that we own, almost—no shit—24/7. I kid you not. There are times when I witness, actually sneak a peek, at my husband *swaying* to the Weather Channel theme music. HE IS SEXY. HE IS MINE.

Which brings me to this. Occasionally I'll get up in the middle of the night and turn on the TV. Unlike my parents, who had a TV in every single room including the extra bathroom, where a small Sony black-and-white sat next to the extra toilet-paper holder, I am not a TV person, as in: there are some shows I watch but can live without. On the occasional night that I do watch TV in the middle of the night, inevitably it goes straight to the Weather Channel, since this was the last channel that was watched. Standing in front of a map of the United States, a perky weather person is pointing up north somewhere and giving a Local on the 8's weather report: *"Tonight in Northeast Pennsylvania we are experiencing a clear crisp lovely evening. Clear as a bell. No precipitation. You won't need a jacket tonight."* As I look out the window from my Northeast Pennsylvania home, I think, geez, anyone can be a weather person because it is snowing like a motherfucker, and *clear as a bell*—hey, you couldn't see the tip of your nose if it were any farther from your face.

AND THEN I HAVE THIS FANTASY: watching this perky person fading, sort of like a dream sequence kind of fade out—and as we fade in, *I, me, am the Weather Person. Dressed in a fabulous black pantsuit (wide-leg flair trousers, no doubt) and opera-length Mikimoto pearls. I look fabulous.* Behind me is the map of the United States, and I, the new, perky, menopausal Weather Person, am covering the Local on the 8's. My show is called "The Internal Storm Outlook."

AS I POINT TO THE EAST COAST:

"Here in Northeast Pennsylvania a major tornado occurred in the home of a woman in her midfifties. When her husband asked her how her day was, she didn't like that he didn't include the word "please," and with that Mary Majors tore her home to bits."

AS I POINT TO THE SOUTHERN STATES:

"We have an unusual storm brewing. It appears that a
menopausal woman was pulling into a parking space and was
blindsided by a disabled vehicle. The woman, whose name is
not being revealed, got out of her car and beat the crap out of
the hood of said disabled vehicle until both the hood and air
bag exploded, leaving the disabled person trapped. When the
cops arrived, the unnamed woman screamed: 'Fuck you! I am
disabled, I am emotionally disabled!' and was led away only
after she was able to call her husband from her cell phone."

AND HERE IN THE MIDWEST,
AS I POINT TO A GENERAL AREA:

"A biblical flood warning is in effect. Two friends decided that
they had had enough of their husbands' bullshit and they let it
rip, opening every single fire hydrant within a ten-mile radius,
and now the entire town is under water. When asked, the local
meteorologist said, 'Well, I gotta tell ya—seems to me it's the
internal storms that cause the most damage.' Leaning into the
camera: "Can I say hello to the little wife and kids . . . ?"

FORTY-SIX

UH, OH

IT IS DECEMBER 31. *We are about to have a New Year's Eve dinner party at our house for sixteen people. Ken warns me that this is the last time we are ever doing this. It makes him completely nuts.* COMPLETELY. Sixteen people, lots of champagne, lots of food, lots of—well, lots. Lots of. And I am cooking and preparing and trying to keep everything in check—why, oh why, someone tell me please why I need to keep everything in check—and I sit down at my computer to find a recipe—*the recipe*—for the shrimp and scallop dish I am preparing, quite badly, I might add, because I don't have some of the ingredients, which I neglected to buy, because I neglected to look at the list I had written before I went food shopping, and there in my inbox is an email from my brother. In the subject line it says something like "MOM'S CONDITION" or "MOM UPDATE." I truly do not remember the exact words that were in the subject line, because my heart started to pound. I open the email and it says something to the effect (not exact words) that my mother *has been* in a hospital for six days and the prognosis isn't good, so if I want to see her, blah, blah . . . blah. BLAH.

This is the email I get late afternoon on December 31—not a phone call, not a phone call days earlier letting me know that my mom is being taken to a hospital. I immediately call the assisted living facility asking why, oh why, hadn't I been called, and I let them know in a clear, crisp voice that my brother and I do not talk at all—something I have never said to them before but feel the need to in this phone call. My brother and I don't speak at all. I am told by the attending nurse when asked if they should get in touch with me—my brother tells them, no, he will get in touch. HE DOESN'T. And I get this email after the fact. Obviously I don't know if this is the truth or not, but I'll take the attending nurse's word. *Maybe they didn't ask. Maybe she is in fact covering her ass.* And having spoken with my mom on the very day that she was hospitalized, I AM SWIRLING AND SPINNING AND MY HEAD IS SPLITTING APART AND I AM HAVING A HOT FLASH, AND I STRIP DOWN NAKED AS I CRADLE THE PHONE AND EXPLAIN TO THE NURSE THE ENTIRE SCENARIO WHILE TRYING TO . . . CRADLE THE PHONE. Everything from how difficult it is to get my mom on the phone to why aren't my calls returned when I leave a message on their inbox/voice mail, and while I'm on this tear, she then—then—informs me that there is a policy at this facility that long-distance phone calls *cannot* be returned. Ken comes into my room, gives me a thumbs-up, and a *"Hey, how are you?"* sort of wave, and gestures to my shoulder, and another gesture that I should maybe use the speaker phone. Uh, huh. That'll make it all better. I am preparing a Happy New Year dinner party for sixteen people and don't have the shrimp and scallop recipe, and (as I cup the phone so the attending nurse doesn't hear me) I tell Ken that he must now prepare everything because I am no longer feeling joyous and happy, and FUCK NEW YEAR'S. And then I tell the nurse into the phone that they should have contacted me, FUCK LONG DISTANCE, and

. . . and I can't believe that my mom was in a hospital, and

no one called me, and this was the second time I found out

after the fact. I ask if she thinks my mom has any time left, because it seems that she is on her last leg from the email. There is a definite silence. I hold my breath. She says, *"She fell, she was quite disoriented. Your mom has dementia. This is a part of the disease. I wouldn't be too alarmed. She's settled back in and resting. Her back is sore. It's really not life or death. It's all a part of the process."*

I am utterly beside myself. And I am naked.

I literally crawl into bed.

Ken crawls into bed with me and holds me. He very gently reminds me—because I am now in devil-doll mode—how funny life is because just a few weeks earlier I was feeling guilty, or not guilty as per the *Encarta* dictionary, that I hadn't seen my mother and was hoping to come to some kind of decision. Looks like *this* could be the decision. I can't really respond to him while my mouth is open semitruck wide. IT'S WISE FOR KEN TO BACK AWAY. I am reminded once again in that moment that menopause "takes no prisoners." I repeat to myself, almost in a mantra, *"Menopause is about giving birth to yourself, menopause is about giving birth to yourself . . . . "*

I am hoping beyond hope that my water breaks really, really, really soon. Ken asks me what did I expect from my brother, since all of this shit has gone down, and I say, *I expect for him to treat me as my mother's daughter, not as the sister who he doesn't like and who doesn't like him. She is my mother, too.*

AND FOR THE RECORD, there is so much shit on both sides that has been ugly and nasty, and none of us—none of us— are faultless. We grew up with this as our foundation. It is not surprising to me that we have landed here.

But, this is the first time in a very, very long time that I actually cry—truly cry, snot nose and all—over this horrible, vile relationship between my brother and myself, because at the end of the day, MY MOTHER IS THE ONE WHO ENDS UP LOSING. Because it's shit like this that makes me retreat, withdraw, and not want to go visit—it is my way of saying fuck you. FUCK YOU ALL.

Ken is trying everything humanly possible to get me out of bed.

I look at him and say:

"Wow, Ken, this is a first, trying to get me out of bed."

It is, as you can imagine,
a very sweet moment.
Ken is so very good at that.

FORTY-SEVEN

MOM—
The Beginning of the End

I AM NOW ON A PLANE HEADING TO NEW MEXICO
to visit my mom, who has slipped into, I have *now* been
informed, *a deep withdrawal and delusion.* I don't know much
about the withdrawal she's experiencing, other than I suspect
she is shooing away the people she doesn't want around
her, which she has done most of her life, and in terms of the
delusion, that, *I am also informed,* seems to go hand in hand
with dementia.

*This was a very difficult decision for me. For a good twenty-
four hours I am completely conflicted, and with that, I of
course decide that I need to pull everyone into this conflict
with me.*

KEN asks me what it is I'M FEELING, what do I feel in my soul—I tell him if I knew I wouldn't be asking. He says well maybe I should go and then just as quickly says well maybe not. But he believes it would be a wonderful healing experience and he supports me 1,000 percent, because he knows if he doesn't say that, well . . . you can just imagine. So it seems he is leaning toward a yes.

MY FRIEND JEFF tells me that it's really more about how I will feel years from now, and if he were me, he would probably go and visit and try to get a massage or two while there: *"It's very important to maintain your own well-being."*

MY FRIEND KAREN tells me to chant and make peace with both myself and my mom, MY FRIEND PETER tells me that whatever I decide to do, to know it will be the right thing, MY FRIEND ROBYN tells me that I should visit my mom but to stay in a hotel, that way I can have some *"down time, along with a good glass or two of chardonnay,"* MY FRIEND MARCIA seconds that, and she wants to know if I plan on seeing my brother. I tell her no. No? No. No? No. I can tell she's a bit disappointed that there won't be a family reunion of sorts. Marcia is a wonderful mother and has a close-knit family.

I move on to MY FRIEND TERRI. Terri tells me she would go with me if she could, but given the financial climate, she can't afford to, but that if she were me she would be on the fence until the very last moment. MY FRIENDS NANCY AND JEANNIE—who are partners—tell me in unison that I should definitely go but not to overstay the visit, because an extra day could add "regret" and the point is to spend time with my mom, love her, and then leave quietly. MY FRIEND DAN, who is going through an almost identical situation with his mother and uh . . . *sibling,* tells me not to go, that I'll only be sad and hurt and horrifically disappointed. But it is my closest friend, MY SOUL SISTER AMY *(Litzenberger),* who gives me the best advice—

she tells me that I should go, bring my mother great joy, love her, expect absolutely nothing in return, and tell her that it's okay, really, really okay, for her to let go. And then Amy says in her wonderful, oh-so-gorgeous voice, which perfectly matches her oh-so-gorgeous soul: "She needs to see you again."

THAT SETTLES IT. I book my flight in the middle of the night, at 3:42 AM. I also book a hotel and google local Albuquerque massage therapists, nail salons, and the nearest Borders and/ or Barnes & Noble.

The only residue of uneasiness that remains lodged inside of me is my deep fear of flying. I have on many occasions refrained from barging into the cockpit, demanding, *"Hey, guys, can you just fly a little slower and stay in one lane."* Maybe it's my need to feel in complete control particularly in an enclosed space, not to mention that I prefer being the driver, not the passenger, and I'm pretty sure it also has to do with the fact that if the plane does go down, I will be with a bunch of people I have absolutely no connection to while being trapped in an enclosed space. But from a Buddhist perspective we are all interconnected and have been together many, many, many lifetimes. It's just in those times, those situations, when I'm on a plane, seated between two people who don't at all feel or seem familiar to me, that the awful, uneasy, queasy fear arises.

On the first leg of the trip (there are no direct flights to Albuquerque) I am seated next to a young woman who is rotating her beautiful rosary beads between her thumb and index finger. She is young and so very lovely and I find myself staring at her rosary beads, and I can tell (intuitively) that this is making her completely uncomfortable, but I'm searching for something, and I find it as soon as I look up at her face: I can sense that she has her whole life in front of her. This gives me great comfort. And with that, I stop staring.

THEN I THINK ABOUT MY MOM, whose life is no longer in front of her—in fact, I believe, although I don't know, all she really has, lives in, is *this very moment.* Which is, per Eckart Tolle, all we really do have—this moment. He does everything in the moment. It's astounding to me what he can accomplish in "the moment." Because I have news for you—by the time I make a decision, or figure out what I'm doing, or decide what to wear, there are a whole lot of moments that have gone by. I don't even know where they went. Maybe there needs to be a friends and family and partner *"extra moment plan"* where you get to save up all those moments that somehow fall into the ether and then you can recapture all those moments when you have the time.

DEMENTIA HAS GRABBED HOLD OF MY MOM AND REFUSES TO LET HER OUT OF ITS GRIP. First the mild stages, the struggle to remember names and faces, the little confusions, the misplacing of the keys, the panic of a wallet disappearing, did I leave my coat at Sylvia's? Then the mild turns to moderate; all the emotional confusion, anger, the sleeping fully clothed with her hand gripping her purse, along with a profound defiance, and the beginning stages of incontinence. It is a difficult stage. It involves a great deal of acting out, and sometimes it's a random attack on a very innocent bystander. Then the further, much deeper and more confusing disassociation, which leads to the blank stares, the painful frustration at the slight and/or familiar connection, which she can't for the life of her place. I am told by her nurse that she has found a permanent "home" on her recliner, where she "lives" all day long; I am also told that depending on the flavor, the Jell-O could very well end up on the wall or someone's jeans. She no longer wants to eat or speak.

I am forewarned in an email from my sister-in-law that it is highly, highly unlikely, as in slim to none, that she will recognize me.

As I stare out the window—looking at some clouds that seem to be in the form of people holding hands, dancing together—

I am hoping beyond hope that I recognize her.

FORTY-EIGHT

B⊙DDHA-F⊙LL

There are times, in the middle of the night, when I just sit in
front of my altar and chant, sometimes for a few minutes, and
sometimes . . . for about an hour. And there are times, in the
middle of the night, when I have a deep sense of calm, peace,
and altruism.

During those times when I am feeling good and strong and
liking myself enough to not care what anyone thinks of me, I
simply sit and pray/chant for World Peace.

However, those nights are far and few between. Generally at
3 or 4 in the morning, you can bet that I'm feeling worried,
confused, frightened, intimidated, fearful, and jittery, so I

find myself praying/chanting not so much to overcome but to embrace those feelings, and as you can also imagine, while I am embracing those feelings, I am trying to fend off the fear that seems to grab me by the throat.

The following are some of my personal prayers/desires and hopes that I have had, or continue to have, with my palms firmly pressed together (and this, by the way, does not preclude World Peace—I like to think of it as the micro within the macro):

KEN'S HAPPINESS, HIS WELL-BEING, AND HIS SAFETY, PARTICULARLY WHEN HE'S DRIVING BY HIMSELF AND NOT PAYING ANY ATTENTION TO THE OTHER DRIVERS (this, by the way, is not something Ken admits to doing). That he work to his heart's content, that he stay fit and strong, that he can tolerate my crazy shit for another month, or two, or three, that he have continuous peace of mind, that he maintain a good, loving, respectful relationship with his son, and his granddaughter, and that he doesn't ask me when or where I bought the pair of boots that are still in their box in the back of the closet because I will have to out and out lie and that becomes a less joyful and much more desperate, stressful kind of prayer.

FOR ALL MY FRIENDS AND THEIR EXTENDED FAMILIES to have good health, much happiness, great good fortune, wonderful and joyous sex, financial security, and peace of mind.

THAT AMBIEN (NOT AMBIEN CR) comes out with a 7.5mg dose, because I am trying desperately to wean myself off the 10mg, and the 5mg doesn't quite make it.

TO AWAKEN TO MY GREATNESS, to inspire, encourage, and help other women do the same.

To become a woman of unlimited self-esteem.

TO FORGIVE, particularly those who have ripped my heart out with their teeth.

THAT GE goes to a hundred dollars a share.

For my mother's suffering to be removed—replaced by pure joy— and that she goes gentle into that good night.

THAT WHEN THE VISA BILL comes it's less than two thousand dollars.

TO LOVE UNCONDITIONALLY, *to give generously, to laugh loudly, to cry uncontrollably, to stand tall, to be big-hearted, to have more patience, less intolerance, to have absolute conviction, to stand up for my friends and for strangers, to tell a bully to his or her face to fuck the fuck off, and for HBO*

to become a basic cable channel, because contrary to their

great, fabulous, sexy ads, it is TV, and given the economy,

none of us should have to pay to laugh, or cry, or pry open our

hearts and souls for thirty or sixty or ninety or one hundred

and twenty minutes without commercial interruption.

FORTY-NINE

CHAIN, CHAIN, CHAIN . . . *Chain*
(Letter) of Fools

I am getting, on the average, six, seven "chain" emails a week that need to be forwarded to at least twelve people, otherwise my prayers/wishes/hopes and dreams will be OBLITERATED. Wiped off the face of the earth. I will have no good fortune, my family will suffer, and I will experience bad luck along with hives for the rest of my life.

This scares me.

Really.

I open these chain emails in the middle of the night, although they arrive early in the day. These are not emails that give me confidence or courage. So, I keep them unopened, and while

I'm deleting, I delete much of the spam stuff and crap that I've left unread because there is really no need for me to open or respond to an email that says in the subject line "Looking to rent a *condom-minium?* Look no further."

And while I am tremendously tempted to delete these chain emails that often say in the subject line *"An angel is looking after you"* or *"You will be blessed for the next forty years"* or *"Don't discard or you'll go to hell"* or *"Open, send and then watch it come back and then resend again, and watch it come back . . . ,"* I don't delete them. I read them. Sometimes I am genuinely moved and touched by the sentiment, but more often than not, I really don't want to send them to six or eight or twelve people. Because I know from experience that when I have done that in the past, a good four or six or ten inevitably respond by saying, "UH, HEY, AMY, DON'T SEND THIS SHIT TO ME."

But the other thing that gets me is that if you do send it to the six, eight, or twelve people, you are promised: good luck, a long-gone dream will manifest, a bundle of money will appear out of nowhere, your arms will become buff, your husband, partner, and/or spouse will reverse in aging, your closet will be cleaned, your apartment or house will miraculously grow three thousand square feet, you will experience memory gain, weight loss, and all your bills will be paid in full for the next five years.

THIS SHIT IS TEMPTING. I am tempted. I am tempted enough to find twelve strangers from my collective social networking groups, blind copy each of them, and then send FROM KEN'S

EMAIL ADDRESS—which, by the way, he hardly ever opens because Ken does not like being online—so that *this* chain-letter email does not come back to me. But the clincher is, you are only given, like, ten minutes to forward to these six, eight, or twelve people or you will have not only ruined your chances of good fortune for the rest of your life but supposedly—across the board—the good luck of all these people you're thinking of sending it to. I am royally screwed. I have ten minutes to locate and choose twelve strangers from my social networking groups who I would like to see flourish emotionally, financially, sexually, and then cut and paste into the body of the email and then blind copy each one and then get into Ken's account, for which I do not remember the password, and it seems obscene to wake him up for such nonsense. But then I think . . . what if. What if something awful, hideous happens to twelve strangers and I feel completely responsible.

I gently—very, very gently—wake up Ken: "HI, HONEY." And I tell him he has to give me his password, because I need to get into his email account, because IT'S AN EMERGENCY.

He says, *"Oh, really? An emergency, an email emergency? What the fuck is that?"*

I make up some crazy wacky story, telling him it's like a fire, and if I don't throw water on to it, it can spread and kill many innocent people.

He looks at me like I'm not his wife, like I'm some lunatic who entered his wife's body. *"An email fire? You are going to put out an email fire? Who are you, Smokey the fucking Bear?"*

"YEAH, THAT'S RIGHT, SMOKEY THE FUCKING BEAR. OKAY NOW? I NEED YOUR PASSWORD."

"No."

"NO? I'M YOUR WIFE—I NEED YOUR PASSWORD."

"No, you are not my wife—my wife has disappeared. You are nuts."

This kind of patter goes back and forth. Password. No. Password. No. Ken lowers his eye mask over his eyes and falls back to sleep. And with that the ten minutes that I needed to ensure that twelve people, twelve total strangers would have fortune for the rest of their lives have passed. And I wait, as only I can wait, for the sky to fall.

It doesn't.

And two days later, I get a residual check in the mail that I never, ever expected.

FIFTY

A CASE OF YOU

I am alone in a hotel room. It is late at night. It is a little after one in the morning here, which makes it almost three in the morning at home. No escaping insomnia.

I decide, because I am alone, to google my first big true-crush love.

It feels sort of like I'm having an affair. It feels forbidden. The laptop is nestled right on my belly—the lights in the room are dim, except for the splash of light coming off the iMac, which gives it a sexy glow. He was my first puppy love, and we were really great friends and then sort of became girlfriend and boyfriend, and this all took place end of year eighth grade, to midyear ninth. *He was a year older than I was, maybe a little more than a year. We were the odd girl and odd boy out.* We shared a deep love for music: the Stones, the Who, Janis Joplin and Big Brother, Eric Clapton, and the Beatles. I loved "White Room," by Cream, he loved "Jumpin' Jack Flash," by the Stones, and I think we both, hands down, hated "Harper Valley PTA." It's also safe to say that "Going Up the Country" was a very cool song to dance to when stoned on Quaaludes, or any illicit drug for that matter. We both had a great passion for Art, Museums, Galleries, and all things Andy Warhol, and we both loved the whole infusion of the vintage-clothing fashion statement—the silk smoking jackets and long silk scarves, the platform shoes, and the sexy, pinched-waist "right to the knee" dresses.

He had a tremendous talent as an artist, and he looked just like Mick Jagger. TRULY. Tall and lanky, sexy, skanky, big thick lips, and I just thought he was THE COOLEST GUY EVER. No one was cooler. I blossomed into a skinny version of Andy Warhol's Ultra Violet: the long curly hair, upper and lower mascara-ed eyelashes and red-hot lips, this during a time when flannel shirts and ripped jeans were the staple. It was sort of like playing dress-up. He called me his Lady Jane. *But that was almost forty years ago.*

Then a year later, I left school and home and got lost for a few years wearing my flannel shirts and peasant blouses and ripped jeans; and he went on his way—off to college.

I never saw him again.

CURIOSITY ALONG WITH A GLASS OF CHARDONNAY GOT THE BEST OF ME, SO I GOOGLED HIM. There were a bunch of guys with his name, because it was a common name, but nothing came up for him that seemed like a match. I was pretty sure he didn't become a *minor-league baseball player* in Maryland, and it seemed highly unlikely that he became a *hairdresser* in Seattle, although . . . you never really know what turn life takes you on. Chances were slim that he became a *dog groomer,* because I remember he wasn't too fond of dogs, or cats, or anything, or anyone that shed. And then the *dance instructor* in Great Neck seemed such a long shot. I was pretty convinced he was not a black *preacher* in Atlanta, nor was he a twenty-three-year-old *skateboard whiz.* Then I googled his name and our hometown, thinking maybe there was something about his folks, and a mention of him, but there was just a little shout-out, nothing special, and some stuff about his mom and dad moving to Florida to retire twenty years earlier, but no forwarding address or info. And if I remember correctly, if memory serves me, there was some chatter that his father had died years ago.

I scrolled a few more google pages, and it was funny, but it felt like he never existed. OR AT LEAST, NOT THE GUY I REMEMBERED.

I was sad.

Sometimes, you really don't want to extend further out or down into your past. But he was special. I couldn't bare

googling to see if he had possibly died, to see if there was an
obituary with his name in it.

I left a message for Ken on his cell phone. Telling him I loved him MADLY, missed him more, and was awfully glad he was my husband.

Isn't that what you're supposed to do when you almost, but don't, have an affair?

FIFTY-ONE

HELLO?

What if she doesn't know who I am?
This keeps me up pretty much all night. The *what if* factor.
And continues to plague me as morning approaches. I shower,
wash my hair, get dressed, a hint of mascara and lipstick, and
leave the hotel.

WHAT IF when I get there she hasn't a clue, and I'm standing
there, and she looks at me, and I look at her, and then there
are ten hours to fill in with blank stares, and long silences, and
nothing to say. *Do I ask how she is? What's new? Do I bring
up her past?* Ask about her family, what if she talks about her
family but never mentions me. What if she tells me all about
her family, her son and daughter-in-law and her grandchildren
but never, ever says I have a daughter, or son-in-law, then

what? Do I stay? Pry? Try to open a locked box? Do I try and ask more questions? Do I engage the nurses who are with her almost continuously around the clock? Will she remember me if I wear something she liked? Maybe if I do that thing with my hair that she always thought was pretty. Maybe if I wear just a little eyeliner with the mascara, instead of going almost fresh faced. Maybe if I wear a piece of jewelry that might spark a memory. Maybe if I bring her some chocolate, milk chocolate, she will recall a time or place, or a happy moment.

These are the thoughts I have as I walk from my hotel to the assisted-living facility. A twenty-minute walk: a short story, a half-hour sitcom, a news briefing, lovemaking, and a manicure with quick dry.

I announce myself at the front desk and am greeted with a general wave of coolness and aloofness *(or maybe I'm just imagining that)*. I am, after all, the daughter who writes to her, calls her a couple of times a week, sends her little gifts and flowers, but DOES NOT visit regularly. Rumor has it (from cousins, relatives, friends of friends of . . .) that I am the inconsiderate daughter, the irresponsible sister, the East Coast carefree "FUCK YOU" sister who does not have a care in the world, who does not know how to, in the words of my brother, FORGIVE MY MOTHER FOR ALL OF THE SHIT SHE DID TO US. I have forgiven my mother, a long time ago—it's my brother that I don't feel like forgiving—not right now, maybe some other time. Ken tells me my brother is projecting. This is the crap I live with. The internal voices that replay on a radio dial that seems forever stuck: the awful sister, the irresponsible aunt, the unloving daughter, the greedy sister-in-law, the ungrateful someone, something.

This is precisely why I don't like walking—

this is why I prefer cab rides.

I am escorted to the second floor, given a code to punch in so I can unlock the door, and enter. The tenants cannot come and go as they please. I walk to her apartment. I let myself in. She is reclining on her chaise. The nurse is there, administering some meds—my mother turns to me, her eyes completely glazed over. *She looks lovely.* Not a stitch of makeup, her hair is gray and fairly long—a big change from the brunette pixie cut, her skin radiant.

And then she turns from me, closes her eyes. I assume she is falling back to sleep.

"Oh my god, my daughter, Amy,"

she says as she looks up at me again. Her eyes a little brighter, there's a genuine spark.

I walk over to her and she grabs my hand and kisses every one of my fingers. *"Ame-chik."*

She always called me *Ame-chik.*

FIFTY-TWO

HOW MY GARDEN GROWS

MY FRIEND SENDS ME AN EMAIL.

He is wide awake, it is 2:37 AM, and he pours his heart out in this email. His relationship of fourteen plus years has come to a screeching halt, and he admits that he is heartbroken, sad, very, very sad, stay-in-bed-with-the-covers-over-your-head sad, because it appears that his ex is moving along pretty well without him. She's in a new relationship, has a new job, a new apartment and he can't for the life of him understand how she can be thriving without him—as he puts it—so fuckin' fast.

I say I understand. But I don't really understand, because I had never, with the exception of my marriage, been in a relationship that long, and the last semilong relationship I had was so completely wrong that I knew on the very first date but managed to stay in it for four years plus. *I know. I know . . . I know.* WHAT WAS I THINKING? I'll tell you, I didn't want to hurt the guy. So, I stayed for four years plus in a relationship that should have ended the first night we went out. And while I feel so unbelievably silly even admitting this, I also happen to know women who have stayed in relationships for twenty plus years because of a WALK-IN CLOSET.

My friend emails me because he knows the chances of my being up at 2:37 AM are pretty definite.

I'm beginning to think it's no longer insomnia or menopause but that my entire internal clock has somehow shifted and I'm on some other time zone where women get no sleep and walk around zombielike. I turn and look at Ken with his brand-new green suede eye mask and matching green earplugs, a smile plastered on his face, and I can't help but think a good gardener doesn't worry if the plants are going to grow. A good gardener doesn't stand over the seeds and wait, and wait—a good gardener makes great soil, plants the seeds, waters the plant, and has faith, *a grand belief,* that sometime within whatever that garden-growing fertile period time is, a flower, or a vegetable, or some green thing will appear, sprout, blossom—and a great gardener knows that some plants, seeds, flowers, vegetables may die, and he or she mourns for a moment and then more than likely will allow the plant to wither, cutting it back when the time feels right.

I'M NOT A GARDENER. I DON'T HAVE THAT KIND OF PATIENCE. TO WATCH THINGS GROW. *Truthfully, this is why our sex life has been somewhat limited these few years.* Ken is not a worrier. I am a "pull it out by the roots" type of girl. There is so much about us that's opposite. I doubt highly if he and I were more similar we would have lasted this long with this much passion.

My friend says in his email that he wasn't very patient with his now ex-girlfriend, maybe that's why she left—he was impatient and feeling pressure, and now he's resentful and doesn't want to get out of bed. *I tell him that I know plenty of women who don't want to get out bed, but never a guy. I just don't know guys who stay in bed with the cover over their head. Not even my gay guy friends. They get facials in a crisis.*

The first thing I ask in my follow-up response email is if he still loves her, because that decides what kind of action you would want to try taking. I tell him if he still loves her he should get out of bed, shower, wash his hair, eat something, and GO AND TALK TO HER. Flowers are a nice gesture, but not the cheap bunch . . . either get an all-white arrangement, or a dozen or so roses, or even an orchid—orchids are sexy and last long and always make sure that the buds are firm. If she doesn't like flowers, *I advise him, then a magazine subscription is always a good second choice.*

I wait awhile for his response to my suggestion and go about my "online" business: read other emails, check on my weekly horoscope (not encouraging, except for one day midweek, and by then according to the astrologist I may end up in a holding pattern due to Mercury being in retrograde), respond to other emails, google some fabulous faraway vacation spots, check on airline prices, and then . . . an email from him, his response:

"No, I don't think I love her anymore, No, I'm not 'in love' with her anymore. Absolutely not. No. A definite no. I'm really pissed and I'm really angry and I can't fucking believe that she actually did this to me. I was sideswiped. We were still living together three weeks ago—all her clothing was still hanging in the closet. She just up and left. Do I love her . . . no, I don't love her, you know what, right now, this minute, this minute, I don't even like her. She hurt me, she didn't tell me. She left me. She made me put wall-to-wall carpet on all the parquet wood floors. I hate carpet. I did that for her."

THEN IN A MEANDERING EMAIL THAT I COMPOSE, I ASK HIM IF MAYBE, MAYBE HE THOUGHT SHE MIGHT BE GOING THROUGH A MIDLIFE CRISIS, because she is in her fifties, and I share with him that I certainly haven't been a day at the beach these past couple of years. And it's so much about "REACTING," and sometimes, most times, it's a bit mindless and thoughtless, and could be mean, very mean, all the lashing out, and sometimes we just really want to *jump out of our skin,* and I give him a sort of mini-rundown of some of the midlife "SYMPTOMS" that I myself have encountered, and as I ramble in my own thoughts and put these thoughts down in an email . . . he is sending me an email simultaneously, which I read before I finish my lecture email, as Ken likes to call them, lecture emails.

He says:

"She's marrying the guy, Amy—THEY ARE GETTING MARRIED."

Huh. That's a curveball, since I of course had this whole scenario laid out. I delete my entire brilliant email and send this to him instead, AMY'S GARDENING TIP:

"You gotta rip this out by its roots. Just yank. That way, there's no returning. And I suggest you buy some kind of liquid weed killer, in a spray bottle, and spray the entire perimeter of your apartment."

I find out a few days later, in a sweet, lovely thank-you email, he did one better—*he ripped up all the carpet.*

FIFTY-THREE

I CAN'T SLEEP

I am anxious, irritable, worried, dehydrated. Maybe it's the stock market. Could be. I don't even look at the monthly statements anymore. Why, what's the point? I like making believe that I have a fake bank account. It gives me a false sense of hope and security. Everyone I know is holding on by a thread, yesterday there was money, today there isn't. Our broker advises me to start peeking at the statements, April, May—a better time, he thinks. *I don't know about you, but the notion of "peeking" at my statements doesn't give me a whole lot of confidence.* I just keep making believe, and along with my Buddhist prayers/ chants, a friend sends me an abundance affirmation, which I reconstruct to my very own abundance affirmation. Which

I think is an okay thing to do because it is my own personal affirmation, one with a pass code and username.

I am a woman of unlimited means and have more wealth and security than I know what to do with and will share all my fortune with those less fortunate, so please, help me if you can get back all the money that is lost. I will be a good woman and donate time to any cause that seems appropriate.

I realize that is not an abundance affirmation at all, more of a plea, or a bartering of sorts. I've never been a good affirmation type o' gal—I always end up meandering and doing a whole nightclub, stand-up kind of *schtick,* what starts out as an *"I will follow my heart and fulfill my greatest destiny,"* turns into a whole long-winded song and dance, and I always feel the need to include others in my personal affirmations, like *I will create abundance and move in the direction of my greatest dream, but I will bring along with me a hundred and two children and adults from the Price Chopper parking lot and I will set aside my dream so they can go bowling for an afternoon and have a nice lunch.* It's called not feeling ENTITLED. Not "entitlement," which I have to come to realize in my abundant wisdom is completely different, a whole other ball of wax—feeling entitled is all about knowing and believing that something is rightfully yours. This is a deep, deep issue for me. Not feeling entitled. Boy, oh boy. . . .

. . . back to my worries, anxiety, dehydration.

MAYBE IT'S THAT EVERYONE I KNOW IS LOSING HIS OR HER JOB, GETTING PINK-SLIPPED, AND IT SCARES THE HELL OUT OF ME. You know why it scares me, because I don't have enough money anymore to take care of all these friends who will one day be living with me because their houses will go into foreclosure. Maybe it's that I don't remember things when I wake up. Like who I had dinner and drinks with the night before. Maybe it's that we now have two cats, which means I will worry in double time about them. And that gives me a huge, pounding headache.

I tell Ken that I am worried, anxious, and irritable. Without missing a beat, this is what he says: *"We can have sex. That'll make you feel better."*

HOW IS IT THAT SOME PEOPLE JUST REALLY DON'T KNOW WHAT TO SAY IN SOME SITUATIONS? Like what my mother said to a friend whose husband died suddenly from a heart attack many, many years ago (this was long before she had dementia):

"I'm so sorry you lost your husband, I know what that's like, I lost my keys."

I decide to vacuum.

FIFTY-FOUR

DEAR JOHN (AMY)

My girl*friend* breaks up with me.

This was completely and utterly unexpected. Actually I could and will categorize it as a shock. One of those, oh-my-god-where-the-fuck-did-this-come-from moments. But . . . on second thought, not really. Not really a shock.

IT ALL BEGAN ON A TYPICAL, AVERAGE SNOWY MORNING.

Ken made his usual pot of robust Bustelo coffee, which for four dollars the 10-ounce vacuumed-packed bag runs rings around any twelve-dollar-a-pound dark roast. Bustelo is the real deal. Cuban coffee. He pours us both a cup (great guy), he reads (I skim) *The New York Times,* and then we sit and chat about our individual plans for the day. I am writing, or making believe I am writing. Ken is going to repair and replace a section of the deer fencing that in fact has been destroyed by some deer trying to get into and then out of our property. He will fix the fence while standing in ten inches of packed snow. To this day I don't see the appeal of doing this. But who am I to take away his little tiny insignificant pleasures. He gets into his Pillsbury Doughboy snowsuit garb, and I go off to my room, I chant, check emails, okay, okay, not true, *I check emails and then I chant*—whew, I feel better, and then I make my morning girlfriend calls. This is a routine. Chit. Chat. Leave a couple of voice mails. One friend in particular hasn't called back in three days.

I leave what I think is a charming, funny voice mail. A long-winded, full one-minute voice mail, but funny and charming nonetheless. The kind of voice mail that I am always, always waving my index finger at Ken for leaving, you know the kind—the rambling, let-me-give-you-every-tiny-detail-of-my-day voice mail, and then I'll ask you the question I needed to ask at the very end of the voice mail along with my phone number in record speed so you'll have to playback the voice mail at least ten times until you get the number right—kind of voice mail.

She, my friend, the one who broke up with me, doesn't return the call, which by the way, at this particular moment, does not feel unusual. This was—is—not a CODE YELLOW or

ORANGE or RED. This was—is—typical. She very often does not return phone calls. This is all a game—*chase me, chase me, chase me, oh, got me*—all a part of her charm, mystique. The withholding, the distancing, the making you sweat it out, waiting for her to call you or email you back, and when she is ready to respond, she will. Or as another mutual friend so wisely observed, this behavior puts her in complete control. I lovingly relinquished control once I no longer felt the uneasiness and queasiness of the continual (my own doing) emotional brain bashing: *Why, oh why, isn't she calling back.*

WHICH BRINGS ME TO THIS: When people don't return phone calls, all this does is creates a whole unnecessary downward spiral of self-inflicted chaos—WHAT DID I DO WRONG, WHAT DID I SAY THAT WOULD PROMPT SUCH SILENCE, *the backtracking, the retracing of verbal steps, the wondering if something was said, something was done, could it be taken back, could it be retrieved*—did she or he or they open the email yet, can I go into the send folder and see in fact if and when it was read, why isn't she or he or they responding, and on and on and on until your head splits open into

seven thousand pieces.

And I would just like to say for the record, before there was CALLER ID, you could call that person and if by chance they answered their phone, and you knew in fact that they were home, then you had something more to spin into butter. *But now with caller ID, all that fun is gone. Everyone knows who is calling.* Maybe it's me, but I sort of liked the surprise of picking up the phone, and hearing a voice on the other end that I didn't expect. The only time now when you don't know who is calling is if it comes up PRIVATE NUMBER, or it's a telemarketer. And . . . and . . . we all lie about this. *Oh, I wasn't home, or I went out for groceries. Oh gosh, geez, I was in the shower and didn't hear the phone ring.* BULLSHIT. We're all looking at the caller ID and saying, "Nah . . . I don't want to talk to her. Him. Them." I've witnessed this with my own two eyes, being at someone's home and the phone rings and they look at the caller ID, and don't answer the phone, and then actually say to the person who called, oh, I wasn't home, I'm sorry I missed your call. Yes. You. Were. *Pants on fucking fire.*

And yes, yes, of course, there are tons of legitimate reasons for someone to not return a phone call. Death is one legitimate excuse. But it can only be legitimate if the person who hasn't called you back is the person who has in fact died. Because as rude as this may seem, people do make phone calls at funerals. They make phone calls, they make business deals, they call their broker, they buy and sell stocks, they rent their apartments, lease cars. It's rude, but it's done. Cell phones have become the new bubble gum.

The only difference is the level of rudeness; you can't stick an iPhone on the bottom of a chair when you get caught chewing someone's ear off. You have to quickly pocket the phone, and begin to you pray that it doesn't ring or vibrate, or go into some weird seasonal jingle.

OKAY, I DIGRESS, AS USUAL—BACK TO MY BREAK-UP LETTER.

I no longer thought anything of it when days would go by when she did not call back. It was her way of taking charge. I didn't take it personally. She was doing it to everyone.

But Ken reminds me this is always a forewarning that one day this will all come to a screeching halt and you will on that day say to yourself, I knew it. I had a feeling. I knew she or he would hurt me, abandon me, turn on me, ignore me, slight me, or just plain old leave me flat, or . . . hanging out to dry.

There in my inbox was an email from her, and in the subject line it says: "re: hello." I just assume it says something like, "Oh, hey, sorry I didn't call you back, we were busy. Blah, blah, blah."

But what I got was a two-page, single-spaced—with added bullet points—*fuck you it's over* letter.

Okay. So I read it, skim it, a once over. And I am absolutely sure this email was intended for someone else named Amy. I'm certain of this. However, I decide when all is quiet, and no one (Ken) is lurking around, I will once again read the email just to make absolute certain that it is in fact for someone else named Amy, and will feel very sad and very sorry for that other Amy, because while I skimmed the email I could tell it was a rather nasty, bitter, no-holds-barred kind of email.

Ken is sleeping. I am not. I get out of bed and go to my room. I turn on my computer. I go to my emails, and I start to feel a bit of tension building up. A rather unpleasant feeling, a squeamish feeling, what I like to call the doom feeling: the tightness in the chest, the lump in the throat, the tightness in the shoulders, with the added pleasure of a rapid heart beat. Uh, oh, I think immediately, this email/letter is intended for me. Now, I'm not so sure I want to reread it. So I read other emails, do some googling, scout some real estate properties in the local area, and I take a deep breath and curiosity finally gets the best of me—so, I open the "re: hello" email.

The first thing I think that crosses my mind as I'm reading, taking in these two pages: oh my god, if this is really me, if who she is talking about is really, truly me, I wouldn't want to be my friend. I would break up with me, too. And I would maybe even get a restraining order. The person she is describing, no shit, is a complete thoughtless, egocentric, mean-spirited awful, horrible freak. This email is filled with such rage and anger and spewing.

I am speechless.

I sit and stare at the computer screen. Since it is in the middle of the night, there is no one I can call, and emailing will not satisfy my need for an immediate instant gratification answer. I am alone. Of course I toy with the idea of waking up Ken, but I don't feel like hearing I told you so. I let him sleep. Although from the sound of it, the freak-o-zoid who my friend is pummeling in the virulent email would in fact pound the shit out of her husband, but that clearly is not me.

This is where all my years of Buddhism come in to play:

The thing we all know deep in our soul is who we are,

especially in the middle of the night, when all is quiet, and

we're all alone with ourselves. We know the truth of who

we are. When I'm lying in bed staring up at the ceiling fan because I can't sleep—I know exactly who I am. When I'm sitting at my computer, and all is quiet, and I'm staring at the computer screen, *I know who I am. I know all my faults, idiosyncrasies, my quirks, all my shit, my nuances, all the little white lies, all the eccentricities, my irritations, my limitations, and all my foibles. I also know every bit of my goodness, my kindness, and my generosity—every bit of it.* And I generally don't mind anyone calling me on my shit. Oh, I may get a bit irrational and emotional, and tell them right to their face to please, fuck off, but I am often in agreement. And I am a mother hen to my own shortcomings.

I TAKE A DEEP BREATH. I respond to each and every bullet point with my recollection, my point of view. A counter-response. And I add:

"And by the way, the woman you are describing in your

email is a bitter, horrible, nasty woman. I wouldn't want

her as a friend either."

And just like my crazy doctor, she, too, is up in the middle of the night, online. She sends me an email saying that I needed to read between the lines, that all of her anger and hatred was in fact from a long time ago, a build-up if you will, and she felt very much like I needed to be put in my place, and that she oh, so badly just needed to "VOMIT" all over me. And now that she vomited, she felt so much better. And that she didn't want to address any of my feelings, because it was she who needed to (her word, not mine) "PUKE."

The image of being vomited on reminds me too much of the movie *Carrie* with Sissy Spacek.

I reply:

"Just please, do me a favor, and kindly delete the previous email. Let me rephrase this: the woman who sent me that email was a self-absorbed, nasty woman, and I don't want her as a friend."

I feel good, empowered. I imagine Ken saying you (as in the collective you, not the personal you) always know this kind of thing will happen. The eventual demise of a relationship, the end of a friendship—the everything-must-go 50 percent off sale. You know it, and you sense it, you just don't listen to it. I feel strong and empowered.

She then sends me another email:

"I'M NOT THROUGH WITH YOU YET."

Uh, oh.

I envision butcher knives.
STOLEN PASSWORD AND PIN CODES.

Empty bank accounts.

DEAD ANIMALS.

Witchcraft.

And vomit, a lot of vomit.

So, what started out as a typical, average, snowy day . . .
turned into a horror movie—or as Ken likes to refer to it now:
Blood on the Snow.

FIFTY-FIVE

OH, HAPPY DAY

May 22, 1993—Our Wedding

The clock reads 1:47 AM.

I am sitting cross-legged in the middle of my room, in the middle of a throw rug, which by the way has very little, if no meaning, whatsoever to me. It is an old rug, one that should have been thrown away—or given away—many years ago, but I was too lazy, and god knows, lazy breeds more lazy. So it stayed, and I'm cross-legged on it, and I pray that I will not develop some kind of bacterial infection from the possibility of whatever might possibly be lurking inside the weave of this old, frayed cat-pissed-on rug. I am sitting in the middle of the rug, in the middle of the night. Some things you keep, some you throw away. This rug went into the "Ah, let's keep it."

I am looking at old, old photographs from old albums, and

piles of photos I have in various manila envelopes, and all

these photos are scattered every which way. I decide, out of complete boredom to rearrange a few photo albums, update my wedding photo album, which I hadn't seen or looked at in an awfully long time. It is amazing to me that *(a) I was so very thin,* and *(b) that Ken seemed to be—hmmmm, what's the phrase—having second thoughts.*

A couple of pertinent bits of information:

Every single couple at our wedding with the exception of Bob and Tony, who are life partners and who have been together for eons, and Panda and Guido (nicknames, not Polar Bears) who have been together forever—oh,

And, yes, my brother and sister-in-law—*all other couples in fact are no longer together.*

DIVORCE, DEATH, UNTIMELY TAX EVASION, INFIDELITY, OH . . . BREAK-UPS, BREAKDOWNS, YOU NAME IT—IT IS IN THESE PHOTOS. In almost every single photo, a full table of couples no longer together. Fifty-two people total, and twenty-two couples—finished, gone, over. If you were at my wedding, chances are, you're either now divorced or on your way to a divorce. Or dead. We had friends who were cheating on their spouses with other friends with other spouses who were cheating on them with other friends, and all of them—WERE AT OUR WEDDING. I'm guessing we had the only wedding party where the bathroom stalls were locked and/or occupied during the entire wedding. And Ken and I knew none of this, well, because we were oblivious. We were getting married, and what I didn't know an hour before our wedding and what

I know now is that one or both of the "soon to be married couple" is going to have some sort of freak-out either before the ceremony, or after the ceremony. And because I am ME, the freak-out occurred during the entire wedding ceremony.

It is called uncontrollable laughter. It took complete hold of

me—like some strange virus, and truly did not leave my system. The minute the nondenominational minister said, "We are gathered . . . " First it was the silent laughter, the quick rapid upper body quivers and since there is no noise coming from the mouth, it just appears to be some shaking and jerky upper body movement, then it starts to circulate up to the throat and eyes, the eyes start to burn from the tears that are streaming down your face from the silent laughter, and then it's sort of like a wild explosion, the jerky body movements, the laughter, the nose running, the certain words that when repeated

sound funnier the second and third time. *It's like hysterical laughter tourettes. And it is unstoppable. Ken had never seen this before, had never witnessed my uncontrollable laughter. He was aware that I had this, this . . . infliction. But it only happened under duress—being trapped in an elevator, in front of a judge for traffic court, and while getting a speeding ticket.*

Nervous, nervous laughter.

But all of this is a blur to me. I had taken a 10mg Valium per my friend's suggestion. I was nervous. Worried. Should I get married? Did I need to get married? I was happy and content as a single woman, I was thirty-eight, my god, I was working and writing and the thought of telling—sharing with—

another person my every single thought frightened me.
I was going to be "legally" sharing my life with another
person. *Did I really need to do this? Was this what I really truly
wanted?* This was my first marriage. This was Ken's third
marriage. I kept reminding myself that the third time is a
charm. I also kept reminding myself that maybe Ken isn't
all that good at being married. THREE TIMES IS A LOT. Two is
okay. Everyone I know, pretty much, is either on their second
or had a second marriage and decided that two was enough.
BUT THREE IS A CURIOSITY. And while I was internalizing
all my fears and worries and questions and applying and
reapplying lip-gloss, Ken wasn't sweating an ounce. Cool as a
cucumber. Handsome in his gray suit, he had such a presence.

*And . . . the kicker, the real kicker . . . I was madly, wild madly
in love with him. And more than that, I really liked him.*

AND AS I LOOK AT THESE PHOTOS NOW OF US SAYING
AND SHARING OUR VOWS—IT IS QUITE APPARENT THAT
KEN GRADUALLY APPEARS MORE AND MORE UNEASY AND
SOMEWHAT FRIGHTENED ALSO, AND AS I NOW REALIZE,
BOY OH BOY, HE SHOULD HAVE BEEN. The way he is
looking at me in these photos is as if he knew he was marrying
a crazy woman who had just been released from a loony bin.
SERIOUSLY. I was laughing so hard it seemed that I would have
a stroke, or worse, a cerebral hemorrhage. Which would have
left me in a coma, and since Ken is not the nurturing kind, I
mean he's very loving and very kind and very sweet, oh god,
so sweet, but not really a nurturer. He would have left me in a
fetal position—right then and there. After seven minutes of my
nonstop laughter, truly, the nondenominational minister said:

"Okay, let's wrap this up—we're getting nowhere here." And then he looked only at Ken: "Is that okay with you Kenneth?" Ken nodded. I had mascara running straight down my cheeks, There is a photo of my dad looking at me and I know what he's thinking: "Oh, dear lord, please watch over Ken now—as you can see for yourself, she's quite a handful." This from a man who was not at all religious, but I believe god—or a higher being—was searched for that day by many people. But not my Ken, the one religion Ken has and has continued to have since I've known him is praying at the altar of the New York Giants.

This was all coming from a place that I never even knew existed.

And clearly I was pretty off the charts crazy nuts with laughter.

We were pronounced husband and wife, and Ken was told to kiss his new bride—me—and the nondenominational minister wished Ken great luck, and offered me a nod, and a gentle pat on my arm and then, with his wife, bolted out of the room so fast I couldn't even offer him a sip of the "congratulatory" champagne.

I went and sat in the "bridal" bathroom—a lovely little private powder room, with all its pretty glass figurines and perfume bottles lined up perfectly, and a lovely spray of white orchids. I sat for a good fifteen minutes. After the laughter wore off, along with all my makeup and mascara, I took a deep, deep breath. It wasn't humiliation I was feeling, I wasn't embarrassed, I didn't feel ashamed, I was filled with wonderment—I wondered. . . .

Marriage? What did this all mean? I loved being alone. I loved having my own space, my own little home, my own bed to crawl into. I loved watching TV (unlike now) at all hours of the night—when I actually enjoyed watching old movies late at night, maybe it was because I was single and loved the boy meets girl, boy loses girl, boy finds another girl, girl finds another boy, but that girl isn't the right girl, and the boy isn't the right boy, and then the right girl appears and the other girl gets dumped and then the two women concoct some kind of master plan, and *I also loved dancing in my living room listening to Aretha Franklin* and closing my eyes and dancing to the beat of my own walkman. I loved the QUIET of my own space and the CLUTTER of my own mind. *And now I had to share all that.* What I loved most about being alone was that I didn't feel the need to inhibit any single part of me while I was alone. I realized—right then and there in the little powder room—*that maybe I had been alone a little too long.*

I had always had this strange sinking feeling that after, oh, I don't know, eight, ten years people just stop having things to say to each other, especially if you're together a lot of the time. I MEAN REALLY, WHAT CAN BE NEW? *How are you?* Good. *And you?* Good. Good. *What you doing today?* Oh, you know, same old, same old. Yeah. Yeah. I think I was petrified that

Ken and I would stop having things to talk about. I was afraid I would become boring. I don't mind getting older. Not one bit. *But I do so deeply mind becoming a bore.*

My niece, who I think was seven years old at the time, my gorgeous little flower girl niece came into the bathroom and sat next to me. She offered her hand. We held hands and said nothing.

I am reminded what my friend's son said to her when she asked—screamed out loud up to the heavens—to no one in particular, "WHAT IS MARRIAGE ALL ABOUT?" when she and her husband were in the middle of a huge loud argument. Her wise young son said:

"It's about having a very special place for your toothbrush right next to Daddy's toothbrush. It's so that those toothbrushes are never lonely. And you can clean his toothbrush and not tell him, and he can clean your toothbrush and not tell you, and that would be very nice. And you'll have clean teeth."

Sixteen years later—
I laugh WITH Ken.

Then.

Now.

FIFTY-SIX

FOOD COURT

I am awake.

THERE IS NOTHING IN MY FRIDGE.
NOTHING.

Something that looks like a lemon
but could be a piece of cheese.

This is our New York City fridge. It is always empty. We eat out or take out in New York. I very, very, very rarely cook in New York City.

In Pennsylvania our fridge is always full, all sorts of full. There is enough food in our refrigerator to make a feast for four, five, maybe six people.

In Pennsylvania, where we live, there is one supermarket—ONE—within a twenty-minute drive, two within a half-hour drive. So, we do all our food shopping in New York City, and then bring it home to Pennsylvania, and don't ever have to leave our house for a good couple of weeks. We have very few restaurants. No take-out whatsoever.

And . . .

THE POINT IS, I can wake up in the middle of the night and make myself pasta puttanesca, or I can whip up some kind of chicken thing, or even make a Thai dish with curry and jasmine rice if I am very hungry and feeling exotic.

Well, okay, maybe not the Thai dish. And the chicken thing just sounded good, unless you're a vegetarian, which I'm not. But still, there is plenty to eat when I'm awake in the middle of the night, when I am home in Pennsylvania.

BUT IN NEW YORK CITY ALL I HAVE IS CHIPS, CHIPS, AND HUMMUS. AND THE HUMMUS IS DEBATABLE. THERE IS NOTHING FOR ME TO EAT.
Oh, wait, Kibbles 'n Bits . . .

So as I lie in bed in the apartment starving, I think: *I have it, I have an idea for women who are hungry, menopausal, looking for a good piece of protein to bite into when they wake up at some ungodly hour,* and I feel brilliant and genius and can't wait to tell Ken first thing in the morning that I have an idea that is going to make us uber-rich:

MENU

PAUSES

Takeout for women, prepared by women

Delivered by women

24/7

No woman ever has to ever settle again
(in the middle of the night)
for just eating her heart out.

FIFTY-SEVEN

CONNECTING THE DOTS

I am awake, thinking I have some kind of brain tumor thing happening, because I am having strange headaches and my face hurts. And it seems to be only one side of my face, and it feels like my face and the back of my skull are going to explode. Maybe it's brain cancer, I think, because that's where I generally go when I'm not feeling all that perky.

LUNG CANCER, BRAIN TUMORS, COLON CANCER, LUPUS, BELL'S PALSY, A STROKE, OR MINI STROKE, ALS, KIDNEY CANCER, IRRITABLE BOWEL SYNDROME, you name it, I've probably at one time either imagined I had it or thought I had it. This is where I go. I have other friends who go there also, and I have found, women much more than men. Some of my men friends go there, but not in the same way. Women go in a full 100 percent. We often compare all our Google notes. Sometimes we even have the same diseases on the same day and wonder if it's an environmental thing, and of course once you go there, you have all these amazing, righteous thoughts about becoming a whistle-blower and bringing the entire toxic town to its fucking knees. And then Meryl Streep plays you in the movie version after the book and foreign rights get scooped up. And of course, the *one-woman play.* And then the PULITZER, and all of this obviously posthumously. And not only are you a whistle-blower, but then you are a martyr.

And even though you're a Buddhist, the Catholic Church

makes an exception and anoints you a saint.

I GOOGLE "BRAIN TUMORS" AND I HAVE MOST OF
THE SYMPTOMS.

Except . . .

For two *major* symptoms, and they seem like the real giveaway. And then of course, they have a few other sites you can connect to, and/or possible links to other head, brain-related injuries or problems.

I spend about an hour online and come to the conclusion, my own medical diagnosis, *that I have sinusitis.*

I can't tell you how relieved I am. Although I am fairly

convinced, at this stage in her career, Meryl Streep does not want to play a woman with sinusitis. It's not juicy enough . . .

unless of course, the sinusitis is somehow connected to some

optic nerve damage, and she ends up blind. And of course,

being a blind whistle-blower has Oscar WRITTEN ALL OVER IT.

FIFTY-EIGHT

THE FINISH LINE

You've all seen this image:

A woman—glistening in sweat—arms held high above her head as she rips through the tape. She is ecstatic.

An ever-victorious smile plastered on her face, along with a double-digit number pinned to her athletic tee.

She has just completed a twenty-eight-mile marathon.

SHE IS MUSCULAR AND FIT AND DELIRIOUS TO THE BONE. After all these months and possibly even years of getting up at 3:00 AM, running, stretching, changing dietary habits, injuries, setbacks, impossible tasks, sprained ankles, marital woes, personal trainers, not to mention sheer and utter determination—all this hard work has finally paid off, and she knows with every fiber in her being that this is just the beginning.

She fought, SHE WON, and she will be training for, preparing for, and completing many more marathons—longer, harder and more tedious marathons. And she knows when she looks in a mirror—whether it be a medicine cabinet, or compact, or full length dressing room mirror—that she in fact has become a fabulously well toned, svelte, perfect size 8 and miraculously fit—emotionally *and* physically—person.

That woman . . . is not me.

HOWEVER, I AM AT THE FINISH LINE OF AN ENTIRELY DIFFERENT MARATHON, ONE THAT BEGAN SIX YEARS AGO. I, too, have spent many a night sweating profusely, maybe not categorically glistening, but there have been a few occasions where I have completely stripped down in public bathrooms. This is true. Using both the coarse brown paper towels and the ever efficient, extraordinarily loud hand blower to dry myself off—head to toe. It has often made me think that yes, there should be a GOLD MEDAL given for gracefully returning to a table—where the ever patient husband and fabulous friends and waitperson are all commiserating.

THIS IS NO SMALL FEAT.

I was born with the umbilical cord wrapped tightly around my neck. My mother claimed I was choking to death. My father countered that the doctor cut the cord before I could've choked to death. *And there is some suspicion that it was in fact my brother who lassoed the cord around my neck.* My mother tells everyone that I came into this world with great determination and spirit and a CUTE LITTLE ASS.

I have often thought having the cord wrapped around my neck was incredibly symbolic. Always being afraid of my own voice.

But menopause rearranged the entire road map—all un-chartered territory. My husband can attest to that. Want to know what I think menopause really truly means?

That women no longer have to punctuate ANY SINGLE PART OF OUR LIVES with a fucking period.

FIFTY-NINE

POST (MENOPAUSAL) SCRIPT

What started out as my journey through menopause—

my wacky, funny, joyous, weird, sad, extremely personal

experiences—somehow, and not at all coincidentally

(I AM AFTER ALL A BUDDHIST), *became a book about*

my menopausal journey coupled/woven together with my

mom's journey and her rapid descent into dementia. THIS WAS NOT PLANNED. Not at all. It was something that just happened. At first I thought, *"Yeah, there she goes stealing my thunder, I have menopause . . . of course she has to have something like dementia . . . "* but menopause, no shit, is a walk through the park compared to what my mom is going through. Dementia is a nasty and uncompromising disease. It has ravaged my mother. *Physically, emotionally, spiritually, sexually, intellectually, and fashionably.* And if you knew my mom, you would realize that the "FASHIONABLY" part is the primary insult to injury. The first thing my mom did when she saw us—her children, or her grandchildren, or any family member—was comment relentlessly on our appearance.

I hate your hair, it's much too short, what's with the frizz, hate the frizz, you're not wearing any makeup, you look like a ghost put on some blush, what's with the T-shirt and jeans, I hate the boots, what are you, a fucking horse trainer. Wear a pair of heels; get the hair out of your eyes. Your skirt is too tight, your pants are too baggy, your sweater is the absolute wrong color, never, ever wear green, it makes you look sickly.

And on and on and on . . .

With dementia she just nods and smiles, saying absolutely nothing at all about appearances, which is probably adding severe heartburn, acid reflux (or is it reflex?), or ulcers to her already deteriorating body for having to keep her strong feelings and opinions all to herself.

I had no idea we would meet here.

IN THE MIDDLE.

Our relationship had been fraught with so much for so long, and it had been just recently that we started relating to each other not as mother-daughter but as friends.

THE THING IS, FOR BOTH MY MOM AND ME, GROWING UP WAS HARD FOR US—I certainly didn't make it any easier on her, and she certainly didn't make it any easier on me. And I made no bones about it, nor did she. We had a tormented, painful relationship. I was rebellious and awful and at times truly hideous. One could even categorize me as a "TROUBLED TEEN" if you must really know, and she was very unavailable, inattentive, and distant—and one could most certainly categorize her as not being a good mother, *at least not a good mother to me.* A mom in name only. This was a match made in biological heaven.

So, this is where we meet.

ME, AT AGE FIFTY-FOUR, AND SHE, AT AGE EIGHTY-EIGHT. She is on the last tour. I am gearing up for a brand-new adventure, tour bus included. She is at the end. I am smack dab in the middle. I could belabor the fact that it took so long to get here, but as my friend Terri so lovingly reminded me, *"at least you got there."*

The last chapter, *the epilogue,* is my tribute to the woman who brought me into the world. We didn't always like each other, we didn't always love each other, we very rarely saw eye to eye, we fought like cats and dogs, we hurled expletives at each other like Frisbees, and we disappointed each other more often than I care to possibly remember. *But as we both grew older, and a bit wiser, and kinder, more tolerant, less combative, we found that we actually liked each other.* Not every day, but enough days a week. And I was deeply comforted in the fact that as I got older and found my way, settled down with Ken, became successful, she was so very proud of me, the life I chose. Because I have to tell you, there was a chunk of time, oh, I'd say between thirteen years old and twenty years old where the life I was choosing was probably very frightening and very unsettling to my mom, my dad, and . . . MYSELF.

But for two days, on my last visit with her, I loved her more than I ever imagined I could, and I finally understood with every fiber in my being the indescribable bond between a mother and a child.

EPILOGUE
DEDICATION

• • •

The following Epilogue is dedicated
solely to Krista Lyons
for encouraging me—
with great generosity and love—
to go deep down inside,

and just dig.

EPILOGUE
Mother/Daughter—Ends Meet

I WANTED MY MOTHER TO BE EMMA GOLDMAN.

Really. Truly.

This only after I saw the movie *Reds*.

Long before seeing *Reds* I just wanted her to be awake when I left for school, or attentive when I was home, or nurturing when I was sick, or available—*just plain available*. But that wasn't who my mom was. She slept in almost every morning. My father would inform us not to wake her. Which meant the need to be quiet—to tiptoe around, to make our own breakfast, or make our own lunch, or have enough lunch money so we could get a sandwich, or a hamburger, or a milk shake at the neighborhood luncheonette. We also had to be quiet on Saturday and Sunday mornings. It wasn't just school days that were forbidden territory—every day, it seemed, was a "Shhhhh, let Mommy sleep" day. Back then, when I was a child, I just wanted my mom to be awake, be attentive, be nurturing—be available.

You know: Just. Be. A. Regular. Mom.

I wanted her to be like all the other moms who lived on our street. Because they would get up in the morning with their kids, make breakfast, be fully dressed with hair done and makeup on and be perky. Perky was not a word I would ever associate with my mom. The one time I recall my mom making breakfast, she was wearing a head full of curlers, a housecoat of sorts, and, of course, in an ashtray nearby, a cigarette burning, as she scrambled my eggs with great disdain and resentment. I didn't want to tell her I wanted them scrambled with just a touch of milk just like my dad made, so I said nothing, and when she handed me a plate with running eggs, I ate them. I remember telling my friends at the bus stop that my mom had made me breakfast as if it was the most amazing thing that could have ever happened. An everyday, boring ritual for them. A miracle for me. The other moms would walk their kids to the bus, wave them off, and go back to their houses and close their doors. Maybe some would get back into bed, maybe some would immediately get on the phone, maybe some would write up their shopping list and go grocery shopping, and maybe some would even get ready to go to work. But I can tell you with great confidence that while all these other women were getting ready to do something else after sending their kids off to school, my mom was probably just circling her REM state. And as I got older, and a bit wiser, I became, through the miracle of television, much more aware of other possibilities in terms of motherhood. I wished for many different types of mother. Laura Petrie, Donna Reed, Mrs. Cleaver, Dobie Gillis's mom, Richie Cunningham's mom, and, of course, Lucille Ball. Although truth be told, I never, ever really thought of Lucy as a mom per se, even though she did have a son. But the one woman I really deeply wished my mother could have been was Emma Goldman. A woman with a great sense of self, a feminist viewpoint, an uncompromising spirit, a point of view, a rebel, a socialist, and whoa, tremendously outspoken. And I also, by the way, after seeing the movie *Reds,* wanted desperately to be Diane Keaton, when she was waiting for Warren Beatty at the train station, or to be more exact, I wanted to be Diane Keaton when she finally, finally saw Warren Beatty standing there on the platform. Diane Keaton's eyes. The love, the joy, the sadness, the releasing of all that fear and worry that he would never, ever return to her, right there, on her face, in her eyes.

Her eyes are glazed over.

She is on the recliner.

On oxygen.

24/7.

The nurses tend to her needs every hour or so. I sit at the foot of the recliner, watching her doze off. She weighs maybe ninety-five pounds. She is wearing a cotton sleep gown. Not her favorite housecoat. She seems so much smaller and tinier than I remembered from my last visit. At one time, my mom, I think, was five foot five, or maybe six—yeah, five foot six. I am almost five seven. She and I have the same body frame. But now she is small, and fragile, and probably if she were standing, she would be even tinier. I am here visiting for two days. Two full days. Twelve, thirteen hours a day. I am staying at the hotel down the road, so I can have a few hours alone, and much-needed downtime, per Robyn's suggestion. Downtime with a glass or two of chardonnay—that's when I call Ken, call a few girlfriends, open emails, read and then write some emails, watch the news, read a magazine article or two, open a book, and try to get some sleep. I sit at her feet and watch her doze off. I am reminded of a life she had, when lying on the recliner was saved for my father. An activity he quite enjoyed with book in hand. You could always find my dad on the recliner, listening to his favorite albums on the stereo, reading one of his favorite authors. And for the record—Ethel Merman, Leonard Bernstein, Billie Holiday, Judy Garland, Philip Roth, John Updike, Saul Bellow, Norman Mailer, Ian Fleming, and James Michener were all favorites of my dad's. He loved to read. And he loved reading in the bathroom. He always read while on the toilet. Rumor has it that one time he went into the bathroom with the book *Hawaii* and didn't come out for most of the morning. When my dad was alive, you would very rarely see my mom on the recliner. She would be in a chair, or on the couch, knitting sweaters, beading flowers (a craft she and my aunt picked up one summer, and for a good portion of July and August, and the subsequent months that followed, they feverishly made every kind of beaded flower you can possibly imagine) always working with her hands.

She loved to knit. She and her sisters would whip up sweaters and scarves and blankets with multicolored squares in record time. And often in a real sisterly competitive way. *"Hey, Gert, I just finished the sweater," "Well, Bea, I just finished a full-length coat," "Well, guess what, girls, I just made an afghan blanket with matching boots and matching shawl and matching sweater."*

He reclined.

SHE SAT UPRIGHT.

He read.

SHE KNIT.

And on occasion, they would do *The New York Times* crossword puzzle together with a crossword puzzle dictionary very close by, usually wedged between them.

She loved being his wife. He loved being her husband. And they had two kids, a boy and a girl, ten years apart, who no longer speak to each other.

I massage her covered feet very gently. Her toes hurt. The nails on her toes are thick and discolored. I remember her going for pedicures every single month before it was fashionable, before there was a mani-pedi place on every corner, on every block, in every single strip mall between Los Angeles and New York City. She always had a pedicure. Red toes. She took great pride in her gorgeous, long, perfect toes.

And sometimes, she would even wear open-toe shoes in the winter, because she knew her feet were sexy. I ask if she would like me to take off her socks, and she shakes her head no and lowers her eyes. She is embarrassed. I understand.

I am reminded by all the photos that surround her of a woman who was beautiful and lively in her day. I can't imagine for the life of me that the woman in those photos, with her family, her husband, her grandchildren, her sisters, her mother, her children—her friends—I can't imagine that she could have ever imagined that this is where and how her life would end up. On a recliner, with oxygen, not knowing who she is or who anyone is, a good portion of the day.

The nurses come in and tell me that they need to "change" her. She has "soiled herself." I step aside, and they try to lift her into a sitting position.

SHE SCREAMS. A sound the likes of which I had never heard.

The only way I can describe this sound is that it's animal like. It comes from her soul, from a place that is so raw and frightened and the only time I had ever, ever heard a sound like this is from the movie *The Miracle Worker,* when Helen Keller screams, howls, at Annie Sullivan in the little house that they are living in while Annie is trying to teach Helen to "speak" some words with her hands. It's that kind of animal sound, and it lasts for almost twenty minutes.

THIS REALLY SCARES ME. They tell me that it's because she is in pain, and it seems to happen when her body moves unexpectedly. She had fallen, she hurt her back, she is in pain—this is the sound she makes because she is in pain. They also tell me that this screaming is a part of the disease, the dementia. I look at my mom, her face is contorted and I see that she's not in pain, this is not pain, this is fear. Absolute, pure, unadulterated fear. It is fear and the inability to say what it is she wants and needs to say. I take my mom's hand and I kiss it and squeeze it, and ask them to please help me take her to the bed, so I can lie down with her and hold her and maybe, maybe, maybe she'll feel a bit safer. A bit better. Less afraid. Or maybe the truth is that this will make me feel less afraid, a bit better, and safer. They lift her on the count of three and move her into the wheelchair, and her screaming persists. I tell her, *"Mom it's okay, it's okay, it's okay."* They wheel her into her bedroom, I am right behind, and as they lift her, on the count of three, onto the bed, she screams louder and deeper, and more. She screams more. Her mouth open and a horrific, guttural sound coming out. I get into bed—lying next to her—I hold her. She cries and cries. And cries. They manage to change her while I hold her toward me, cradling her. They clean her and wash her, and cover her with her favorite blanket all while I hold her—she squeezes my hand. She says to me: "You are such a wonderful letter." Letter, I think, letter—what does that mean? Is it because I'm a writer? Maybe that's it. The nurse whispers, *"Daughter, she means daughter."* Somehow the thoughts and words can't and don't come together. Letter is close enough, I think to myself. Letter, daughter; daughter, letter—I can see the connection. I tell her that she is a wonderful envelope. She nods, laughs. The nurse tells me it appears that she understands.

Maybe.

Maybe, I think as I stare up at the ceiling, maybe she should have stayed in Florida. A big, taboo *"Let's not talk about this, because if we talk about this, there's going to be a lot of shit said that we're all going to regret, but never really talk about, because god forbid there's a confrontation in the moment we're all feeling the need to express ourselves, so we'll keep it inside and never, ever talk again, that'll be much better"* subject. I know this for sure. My brother wanted my mom near him, so he could take care of her, to be there if anything happened, and once he made up his mind, he was perfectly clear about it. A strong, adamant decision. He's very good at making those kinds of decisions. The ones that seem to have no, or little, wiggle room. It works for him. I need a lot of wiggle room. A therapist would call it a fear of commitment or possibly a loosey-goosey way of life. Works for me, but not so much for Ken. My mom wanted to be taken care of. She had been taken care of her whole life. First by her three older sisters, then by my dad, and now by my brother. I wonder somewhat out loud, to no one in particular, if she had stayed in Florida, stayed in her house, had round-the-clock care, would she have fallen so rapidly into complete and utter oblivion. A question—to really no one in particular.

Yes, probably, I think. Probably she would have. She would have fallen into a deep, deep oblivion. No matter where she was. Dementia doesn't pick and choose its final destination. I am holding her. There is not much to do since the TV in her bedroom is not on and the remote is nowhere to be found. It appears she would like to fall asleep. Her screaming has stopped and she can breathe easier. There is a quiet, a calm. The screaming knocks the wind out of her. And just hearing her screaming knocked the wind completely out of me. The nurse tells me that in a few hours, it will start up again. The screaming. In a twenty-four-hour period, they tell me, she can scream four, five times, for twenty minutes a pop. But for now, she is quiet. The nurses leave us alone. I stroke her hair. She loves her hair being stroked. This is the first time I can remember that my mother did not have hairspray on her hair. It is soft and silky and as I run my fingers through it, she "ahhhs" and "ooohs," and my life memories flash by as if they were Technicolor *web-i-sodes*.

Little vignettes of different times and places.

There is a framed black and white silhouette of me from when I was in kindergarten on the opposite wall from her bed. Hanging right next to a lithograph. It sparks a curiosity since I am wholly aware that there are tons and tons of photos of my brother and his family, many old photos, many recent photos, both hanging on the walls throughout her apartment, and lined up neatly on her shelves . . . and among all those photos, there are only a couple—a handful—of photos of Ken and me. I can recall just two. One from our wedding, where amazingly I am not laughing, and the other from when we visited my folks down in Florida, sitting underneath some kind of tiki hut—Ken and I look completely out of place. And then there are two photos of me, one when I was a young woman, the other one holding my nephew when he was a baby. But there on the wall across from her bed, framed, is a black and white silhouette from when I was five or six.

It hung on the wall in our den when we lived on Long Island. I remember having lain my head down as all the kids in the class did on a piece of black construction paper, and our teacher, Miss Cherry, outlined each one of our heads along with the outline of our hair—mine, in a long ponytail—in white chalk, and then cut the silhouette very carefully and precisely with a scissor, and all the kids brought these home for our parents as a special gift for Valentine's Day. I also remember not long after this silhouette thing happened, my next-door neighbor (who was also my girlfriend, and shall remain nameless, as to not embarrass her now, later in life) wanted to play beauty parlor. Coin flip. Tails I was the beautician, heads I was the client. I got heads, and the next thing I knew I was carrying one of my pigtails home with me in my hand. Just to imagine the whole visual effect of this, I wore my pigtails high up and very tight on my head. My mom made the pigtails so tight my eyes actually hurt. In a massive rage, my mother grabbed a scissor and cut the other pigtail right off, leaving me with huge bald spots, and then cut and chopped the rest of my hair in some sort of strange, dicey mess. She forbade me to ever play beauty parlor again with my nameless friend. It didn't seem that was going to be very difficult a request. (a) I had no hair, and (b) I had no hair.

I started playing potsy (or hopscotch, depending on where you're from). That was a game you could play all by yourself. All I needed was chalk and a sidewalk.

My mom loved that silhouette of me. When they moved from Long Island to Florida, it went into the guest room, and when she moved from Florida to New Mexico it went into her bedroom. Although I suspect that she had little to do with any of the wall-hanging arrangements.

She opens her eyes.

She smiles at me.

She asks if I like to sing. I say yes, sometimes. She tells me, matter-of-factly, that she was an opera singer. I know this is not true, but I say, "Yes, I know." And the reason I say this is that my friend Patricia tells me that there is no point whatsoever in trying to convince a person who has dementia or Alzheimer's that they are in fact fabricating a story. It's sort of like trying to tell Ken that he needs to drive slower. They just don't hear you. Period. She tells me she was very, very, very famous. This makes me think of the Facebook exchange with the woman who confused me for someone she went to Vienna with, who thought I sang with her in the Vienna chorus. Life is funny that way. My mom asks me who my favorite singer is, I say Laura Nyro. "Oh," she says. "I don't know her. Is she pretty?"

Growing up, I played Laura Nyro every single day without missing a day for about a year straight. Every single morning, and every single evening until I wore out both the grooves in the albums and the welcome in my own home. I loved Laura Nyro. I wanted to be Laura Nyro. I wanted to play piano and wear long flowing black dresses, and sing about the Poverty Train, and Sweet Blindness, and Time and Love (*everybody*), Emily, and Oooh, la la la, Oooh la la, I wanted to have a head full of long wavy thick hair, and sing about Eli and the Thirteenth Confession and New York

Tendaberry. I also after reading the biography of Malcolm X wanted to be a black male Muslim, but somehow, I didn't think that would go over quite as big given my upbringing, nor did I think the chances of my becoming a black male Muslim were nearly as good as my becoming Laura Nyro, even though I couldn't carry a tune.

My mother really didn't "get" her. She thought her lyrics were depressing and dark, filled with longing. (Oh, my god, could you imagine if I had played Jethro Tull or Frank Zappa incessantly?) She reminded me consistently that she was in fact a very bad, bad, bad influence on me. Until one day when the 5th Dimension, who my mother loved, came out with a hit single, "Stoned Soul Picnic," written by none other than yes, that's right . . . my very own Laura Nyro.

For approximately one week, I could do no wrong.

She takes my hand. She likes my nail polish. A very light hint of pink. I tell her it's called "Sold Out Show." She often wore that color on her fingernails. She doesn't know what I'm talking about. I remind myself if she doesn't remember names and places, why, oh why, would she remember nail polish color.

I wonder if she wanted to be an opera singer. Maybe this was something she wanted to be, but never had the chance, or never felt she could pursue it. I do know that my mom wanted to be an artist, she loved painting and drawing, and boy, oh boy, was she talented, she had a god-given talent that she never pursued and gave up. She gave it up. For me. For my dad, and for my brother. I don't think she would tell you that she gave it up, I don't think she would say that, but I think she longed to be creative, and often she would paint in the den, her canvas on an easel. A hobby. And I do recall her singing in the shower, and singing along with the radio, and all the Broadway show albums that she and my dad loved playing, and I remember, boy do I remember, that during every summer, they would put on all these variety shows with all their friends and she would sing—sometimes a solo, sometimes in a group—but I also remember that she in fact cannot really carry a tune. Not really. It wasn't that she had a bad voice; it was just that she couldn't sustain the note. And I do remember that she loved whistling. Boy, could she whistle. Another thing she did really, really well was dance. She had great rhythm; she could have been a dancer, any kind of dancer, but most definitely not an opera singer. And aside from not being able to really sustain a note, she didn't have the patience or the discipline to do anything that required a minimum of a few hours a day daily practice or ritual. She truly gave new meaning to the words "instant gratification." She wanted it now. Right now. And if it couldn't happen right now, well, then, fuck you. Next.

She stares at my middle finger on my right hand, then takes the finger and kisses it, then rubs it, and strokes it gently. It has been broken for forty-four years. It is crooked and misshapen. I was ten years old, and we were at the Bungalow Colony for the summer, where we went every single summer from the time I was born—it was our family and my Aunt Gertie's family, and we shared a bungalow. And before I was born, my brother and my other cousin also went to the bungalow, but they were older now, my brother was twenty years old, and I'm not sure where he was, and I'm pretty sure my cousin was married, and living in Brooklyn, and she and her husband would visit on weekends. We—six of us—shared a two-bedroom bungalow, a small, cramped two-bedroom. I slept in a single spool bed in the bedroom that I shared with my mom and dad, and my cousin slept on the porch, on the couch, which was really a bed but doubled as a couch during the day. And the only difference between the bed and the couch was during the day it had a white (with trim) chenille bedspread draped over it. This porch was somewhat connected to my aunt and uncle's bedroom, or seemed connected to my aunt and uncle's bedroom. Maybe there was a screened-in window. I vaguely remember that.

I was ten years old, I was playing with a group of my friends. running, being crazy, laughing, having fun, and then all of a sudden one of the kids fell on me by accident, and he landed right smack on my hand, and my finger curled and snapped. We all heard the finger snap, and the pain was unbearable. I ran straight up the hill to my mom, who was playing mah-jongg with her girlfriends, including my aunt, and I was screaming and howling, and in excruciating pain, and all the kids were running up the hill with me, behind me, following me, and when my mom saw me—she was in the middle of a mah-jongg play—she didn't get up from the table, because she wanted to finish her hand. She gestured, a big, sweeping get-in-the-bungalow-now gesture, and I ran inside, and I kept wailing, and the other women seemed much more concerned because I could hear them talking to my mom about my "hysterical crying," and my aunt seemed the most concerned, and then one or two other kids started crying, because, well, when you're ten years old, you always do what someone else does, and then my mom finally got up from the card table and came into the bungalow. I showed her my finger, which at this point had swollen to about four times its normal size, not to mention my hand blowing up and looking completely unrecognizable in both size and shape, and she opened the freezer and pulled out a metal ice tray and snapped it open with amazing force, and the ice cubes flew everywhere and she cursed, *shit, shit, shit*, and told me to grab a cube, and hold it on the finger, and then screamed for my aunt Gertie to come inside, and Gertie came running in, and my mom asked Gertie if the ice cream truck had come yet, and Gertie said no, and my mom said, when the truck comes they need to *buy two*, not one, but two Creamsicle pops. Then, she put my hand in a large bowl of ice, and told me—warned me—not to move from the bungalow. She went back outside to finish playing mah-jongg. After the ice cream truck came, she walked in with the two ice cream pop "sticks," making a splint for my finger, with some sort of Scotch tape thing to hold it all together.

Later that night, while my mom and dad and aunt and uncle were playing cards on the porch, I lay awake in bed, my finger throbbing in the make-believe splint and my hand swollen beyond recognition, I could hear Ethel telling her husband, Irving, as they walked right past the bedroom window, *"If it were my child, I would have taken her to the hospital immediately, right away."*

My finger never healed. And I've never learned, or wanted to learn mah-jongg, even when it resurged during the whole backgammon craze. She strokes my finger. I believe, or at least I hope, that she knows that she should have taken better care of me.

SHE IS THIRSTY. I ask her if she wants some juice or water, She says water, yes, water, I get up out of bed, and fill a glass, and bring it back to her. She pats the bed, so I get back in. She has a few magazines on the night table, on her side of the bed.

She asks me to read to her. She loves magazines; clearly this is both a craving and a habit that is passed down from one generation to the next. When we moved my mom from Florida to New Mexico, in cleaning out her apartment, all her drawers, and closets, there were tons and tons of magazines piled, some dating back to the late eighties. Magazines that are no longer even in print, they'd been out of print for years. We obviously share in this addiction. I ask her if she would like for me to read her a few articles from a magazine. A strong, hearty *thumbs-up*. Her eyes twinkle. She lays her head on my chest, and I read out loud. First a story about conjoined twins, which is very, very sad and, truthfully, a bit unsettling. There is something about conjoined twins, and please forgive me if in fact you have given birth to conjoined twins, but when one wants to be a doctor and the other wants to be a professional ice skater . . . it's pretty hard for me to imagine how this will in fact happen. I do believe that anything is possible, I do, but I try to envision this whole scenario, does one twin go to medical school during the day, and then the other takes ice-skating lessons at night, and what happens to the twin who doesn't want to skate? I mean really, what if one twin wants to get married, and the other one doesn't. How does that work? I'm figuring one of these twins is not going to fulfill their dream. But far be it from me to discourage anyone to go after what they want. Still, this is a curiosity to me, sort of like tornadoes and trailer parks. And then of course I read something about Angelina and Brad, and their brood, and then something about Jennifer Aniston, and then an article about Brad coming to Angelina's defense because of an article where Jennifer was a bit snarky about Angelina, and my mom seems to really like all the Angie Brad Jennifer crap. Then I read a few books and movie reviews. She loves movies. She and my dad went to the movies all the time. She loved Twizzlers, and he loved popcorn with butter, and chocolate, anything chocolate. Followed by a Diet Coke, and/or 7UP. He loved action flicks and thrillers; she loved romantic comedies and love stories, and they both loved James Bond. 007. Sean Connery, Roger Moore, George Lazenby, Pierce Brosnan, Timothy Dalton, and now, of course, Daniel Craig. My dad loved Sean Connery, my mom swooned over Pierce Brosnan, and my guess is they would both, hands down, be nuts for Daniel Craig. Or maybe that's just me.

She starts dozing off. I read another article—this one not out loud—about a very famous actress who admits to having tried to commit suicide when she was a teenager. She was sad and lonely and felt completely hopeless.

My mom has fallen asleep in my arms.

I had taken an overdose of pills. I knew it was accidental because shortly after I swallowed all the pills, I ran downstairs to the den, and told my dad, who was on his recliner, reading a book. I had swallowed a whole handful of Seconal, the Seconal that he got from his dentist because he had had a root canal and was in tremendous pain. I was overwhelmingly scared. The minute I swallowed them, I knew—I knew—what I had just done was horrific and awful and frightening, and I regretted it. Deeply. It was just I was so sad, and so profoundly unhappy, at that uncomfortable stage at the beginning of being a teenager who had the "weight of unbearable" resting right there on my shoulders. I was tall and skinny and wore braces and had curly, frizzy hair, and some of the kids at school called me Margaret, because she was Dennis the Menace's neighbor and she was skinny and wore braces, and if I remember correctly, no one—no one—liked her. They rushed me to the hospital, the emergency room, where my stomach was pumped, what a vile experience, swallowing this crap that makes you throw up until you feel completely and utterly empty. Painfully empty, all your bones and throat and body aches, and the attending physician—the emergency room doctor who pumped my stomach—recommended that I see a therapist. My father was mortified. He was sobbing. My mother was humiliated and in deep, deep pain. *What will the neighbors think?* I know that was what she was thinking as we pulled into the driveway because a few of our neighbors were watering their lawns when we left the house in a mad rush.

They blamed each other.

I could hear them screaming from my bedroom, where I was resting. He told her that I was unhappy and that he could tell from looking at me that I was so sad, she said, *How the fuck would you know, you're never home,* and then he said, *I work, Bea, I go to work,* and then they got into this huge screaming match, and the fight got louder, which was not at all unusual. They fought all the time. Loud, screaming fights. She would walk out of their bedroom, slamming the door. He would go sit in the living room, in the dark, in the oversized chair that was tucked in the corner, his arms folded, smoking incessantly. One cigarette after another, like a chimney. She would badger him over and over and over. More doors would slam. And then shortly after all the kicking and screaming, and yelling and fighting, they would make up. I would hear her walking down the staircase to the living room where he would be sulking— my dad was a sulker—in his chair, and I would sneak out of bed, and stand on the top of the staircase, where I would get a peak and watch them kiss. And he would say I'm so sorry, and she would say I accept your apology. Two very emotional, and extremely volatile people.

I didn't want to die.

I really truly didn't want to die.

I WANTED SOMEONE TO PAY ATTENTION.

The therapist said, after a few sessions, that he didn't think I felt loved. I told him I didn't know what that meant really. I told him that I felt different, like really different. He asked me what I meant by different. I said I felt special, but I wasn't sure anyone else felt that way about me. He asked me why I felt special. I told him I didn't know why, but when it was late at night, and everything was quiet, and I was all alone with myself, I knew, *I really knew,* that I was someone special. I think he thought I was nuts. Like really, crazy certifiable nuts. After a few more sessions, I began to think that there was nothing particularly special about him. I told my parents I didn't want to see him anymore. He told them he was sure I needed many more months of therapy. He recommended I read some books, *I Never Promised You a Rose Garden* and, if I recall correctly, *Go Ask Alice.*

I didn't read those books. I read Herman Hesse's *Siddhartha* instead.

I mailed the therapist a copy of that book and along with recommending he put this on his reading list, I also wrote—in perfect penmanship—that he was completely wrong about me, that I was, in fact, special.

I lie there, thinking about how sad I was as a child. Sad and lonely, and god, did I feel out of place in the world. Completely. When my mom wakes up I ask her if she remembered how sad and lonely I was as a child. She shakes her head. She can't remember. She doesn't seem to know who I am in that moment. Her eyes are blank and empty. There is no twinkle. Then she tells me she feels lonely now. A dark kind of lonely, she says. I can only imagine. It must be excruciating losing so much so fast. She asks me if I like ice cream. And before I can answer, she says sometimes they bring her some chocolate ice cream, and it makes her feel not so lonely. I don't quite get the connection, until I realize that chocolate—chocolate anything—was my dad's all-time favorite flavor. I miss him, too, I tell her.

SHE DOESN'T KNOW WHO I AM.

The screaming starts up again. It's not quite as jarring. It seems to follow any sort of unexpected movement. When she tries to lift herself up, or she needs to shift her body weight. Any kind of movement is accompanied by a scream.

I hold her and tell her *It's okay, it's okay, it's okay.*

The nurses come in—I imagine they can hear the screaming in the hallway—and tagging along with them comes my mom's "neighbor," who is in a major panic that someone is "howling." It sounds like a murder, she says, like someone is getting murdered. They calm her down, and tell her it's okay, to go back to her room. She stares at me, and then asks me, *"Who are you?"* I tell her that I am Bea's daughter. She asks,

"Bea? Who's Bea?"

I point to my mom and say, "This is Bea."

The neighbor says, "No. That's not Bea. I'm Bea."

The nurse says, "No, honey, you're not Bea."

"I am Bea," she shrills and then slams the door behind her.

She has Alzheimer's.

They give her a sedative. A pill. I ask what it is, they don't tell me. Maybe it's a pain pill, they say. But only the doctor can tell me. Rules. Fucking rules.

She wants to get out of bed and back to the recliner. On the count of three . . . in the wheelchair. The screaming persists. Spurts of screams. But because I now know this is not something I need to be worried about, within the context of the big worry picture, I am more at ease. Less fearful. She screams as they wheel her from the bedroom to the living room. On the count of three, they lift her onto the recliner. It is now dinnertime. Although it feels a bit on the early side for a meal. She says she is not hungry. I tell the nurse if she gets hungry I will go and pick up some take-out from the California Pizza Kitchen, which is only a few blocks away. She calms down. The sedative–slash–pain pill seems to be working. My mom is not at all recognizing or familiar with me, she can't seem to place me, or where she knows me from. She stares at me blankly. There seems to be no Bea there. But she tells me that she likes my hair (thank god) and comments on my wide-legged baggy trousers. Roomy, she says. Yes, roomy, I answer. Very. Could fit both of us in here, I say. One nurse sort of laughs, but my mom hasn't a clue what I'm talking about. Both nurses leave. She dozes. Her phone rings, which is very strange and weird since it hasn't rung at all since I got here. I answer, maybe it's my brother or sister-in-law, or her sister who lives in Indiana, who occasionally calls, so I answer the phone, and it's some fucking telemarketer asking me if I'm Beatrice, I say no I'm not, she asks if Beatrice can come to the phone, it's a very time-sensitive important phone call, I ask how time-sensitive important, she says very. I tell her perhaps she should relay the message to me, and I will make sure that my mom gets it ASAP. She says, and I'm dead serious, that my mother has just won a three-day, all-expenses paid trip to Lake Tahoe to look into a time share, do I think my mother would be interested in possibly this kind of investment. I tell her that my mom has dementia and the chances of her remembering what a time share is in the first place is probably slim to none. I ask them to please remove my mother from their call list because god forbid she has a coherent lucid moment just at the same exact time they decide to call back because these folks are known to call back over and over and over, and she, my mom, might end up saying yes to something she most definitely, without a doubt, needs to say no to. Well, she says, this is a tremendous opportunity, a once-in-a-lifetime kind of offer, and she is missing an amazing chance to have an all-paid-for, *albeit with strings attached,* kind of memory that will last a lifetime.

Whoa, I tell her, whoa, I'll make a deal with you. If you can give my mom back some vital and significant brain cells, and a good solid memory bank, not to mention a real strong sense and clue as to who she is, along with this weekend time-share thing, I would personally consider taking them up on this because then it would be categorized as a once-in-a-lifetime miracle, but if it's just a three-day getaway thing, with strings attached, I doubt highly we're talking once in a lifetime.

I tell her to please have a nice day and to take my mom off their call list now. Right now.

My mom is hungry. I tell her I'll be back in a half hour. She says okay. I bring back some pasta with pesto sauce, a salad, a shrimp cocktail, and some rice pudding, which, if I remember correctly, she likes. I feed her. She hates the pasta. Spits it out. She likes the tomatoes. She loves the black olives and cucumbers. I eat the pasta, and neither one of us eats the shrimp cocktail or rice pudding. Ken would tell me I wasted money.

"Kids are starving in Europe, if you don't eat, if you don't finish what you're eating, we're going to pack it all up and send it to those kids," my mom says at the dinner table, "who, by the way, would give an arm or a leg, or both, to be eating anything right now, because you know what they eat, they eat mud. You wanna eat mud, 'cause that's what they eat and I can tell you right now, they're not complaining. So, you either finish your food, or we send it to Europe, and then I'm not feeding you anymore."

I finish my food. I win the clean plate award, and then I tell my mother that kids are starving in Hempstead. Hempstead, Long Island. She wants to know how I know kids from Hempstead, since it's an all "negro" community. I leave that one alone.

I sort through a box of photos, ones I haven't seen before. Tons and tons of photos, while my mom is reclining, lounging, sipping water from a straw, and watching cartoons. She has found great solace in the Cartoon Network.

The thing about photos, they jar a memory, a moment, a time and a place. Some photos seem so outdated you can't possibly for the life of you recall any of it. When was it taken, where was it taken, and why, oh why, was it taken in the first place? I find photos—Kodak moments. HERE'S ONE:

Me, wearing what appears to be a huge frizzy afro on my head. My hair is so big, it's hard to find my face. I look like a cross between Phoebe Snow and Angela Davis, and from the looks of it, not a very happy Phoebe or Angela. I am wedged between my mom and dad, and it appears that the photo was taken in front of the Dunes Hotel, in Las Vegas, circa 1970. My folks were on a gambling junket; I took a weekend pass from the commune in Oregon where I was now living. I got on a Greyhound and joined them for two days. (And just for the record, that bus trip, from Oregon to Las Vegas, was one of the worst experiences I have ever had in my entire life. There was a sick child who projectile vomited, there was a faux [as in fake gun] hold-up at a rest stop, there was a flat tire, and there was no toilet, and there were seven more hours added on to this already interminable bus trip.) I am wearing, along with this afro do, a peasant blouse, torn jeans, and what appear to be, although I'm not 100 percent sure, huarache sandals. My mother looks very unhappy. My father looks stunned. And I looked stoned out of my gourd.

I dropped out of high school and left home.

This is where I ended up, a commune in Oregon. Trust me, this was not something a Jewish girl from my neighborhood on Long Island did. We did not drop out of high school and go live on a commune with fifteen, sixteen other people, most of whom we didn't even know. We went to Ohrbach's, and A&S, and Bonwit Teller, and went bowling, and played tennis and went to the beach clubs, and never, ever gave blow jobs. Never. Jewish girls never gave blow jobs because Jewish girls did not believe they needed to work. Anything job related was out of their realm. Jewish girls did not announce at the dinner table that they were quitting high school to find themselves. The only place a Jewish girl could possibly find herself was at the shopping mall. And one more thing that Jewish girls did do, and usually did secretly behind closed bathroom doors—they would shave their legs. And when Nair—a depilatory that made your legs silky and smooth—came out, there was a brand-new god in town. Bye-bye, Daddy's double razor. Hello, Nair. The first time I ever shaved my legs was in my mom and dad's bathroom. I did this on the sly. I used my dad's Gillette razor, along with his shaving cream, and proceeded to scrape tiny pieces of skin right off my legs. Each leg had at least twenty-five little pieces of toilet paper attached to the nicks and cuts from using a razor that I did not know how to use.

Which brings me to this: Living on a commune, one does not shave their legs. It's sort of like a rule, a law. You let every single hair on your body grow. One goes au natural—it's part of the whole "communal" experience: being a hippie, living off the land, wearing no panties, no bras, all this free love and absolutely no underwear. And an added benefit, one can even pray daily at the little outdoor homemade "equipped with candles and incense" shrine to "the gods of the sun and the moon, Grace Slick, and of course, The Grateful Dead." I prayed consistently and daily—because I do believe that cotton panties can save you from many unwanted unpleasantries—I prayed to never, ever get a urinary tract infection.

I went to Oregon with my friend—a hippie, groovy musician—who was a sort of boyfriend, but not really, but we pretended to be boyfriend and girlfriend. I think we just both wanted out of Long Island. I had already experienced my first big puppy crush, and like most crushes, it began to fade and then disappear and I was back to square one. And my hippie, groovy friend had his heart broken by some girl who wanted him to drop the whole music thing and go work at Fortunoff so he could get her gold jewelry at a steep discount. So, off we went, my sort-of boyfriend, but not really, and I, to Oregon. His brother was living on the commune and it appeared we had an open invitation. You can just imagine how my mother reacted to my dropping out of high school. She announced to her friends and family that I had died, and she sat shiva. My father, on the other hand, said, "I can't make your mistakes for you, god knows I wish I could," as he drove me to the airport so I could get on a plane to San Francisco, with my massive and heavy backpack, where I would then meet up with my hippie, groovy friend who was already in Oregon, and then we would hitchhike up to Oregon, because, well, if you're going to live on a commune, might as well start off on the right foot, with a thumb out.

I wore an afro, and long skirts and peasant blouses, and ripped, torn Levi's and Frye boots and never, ever shaved my legs or underarms. And we would all sit around, Indian style, myself and all these other women and I would look at their hairy legs and hairy underarms, and think to myself, this just doesn't work for me. I like smooth and silky. I do. Why am I depriving myself, why am I growing hair on my body that I really don't want grown? Why, oh why? *Please, Grace Slick, please, Jerry Garcia, please someone help me.* And then it happened: I was caught shaving my legs—razor in hand, leg propped up on the sink—and the next thing I knew there was a group, a small group standing outside the bathroom door, and I knew that I had crossed a line. I was asked to leave the commune for not following the communal rules. No sense protesting. I was guilty, and I took full responsibility for this heinous and atrocious act. I decided I did not need to present my case in front of a communal tribunal. *"Oh god, yes, I shaved my legs, and guess what, guys, every single day that I was here—hold on to your seats—I wore a hint, a tiny little hint of mascara. And on occasion, a splash, a quick splash of Jean Nate."*

I was not cut out to live on a commune. And as I look at this photo, I can honestly say that this particular stage was not at all becoming. It was my least favorite of all my rebellious stages.

She asks me to massage her legs.

Her legs, she says, feel very stiff and very dry and could I please rub them.

She likes her legs to feel silky and smooth.

I get the Nivea cream that sits on her night table; she loves the thickness and creaminess. There was a time, not too long ago, when she would wear both a floral or fruity or musky body lotion mixed with a perfume or cologne that had a distinctly different fragrance, and the two scents combined—the body lotion along with the perfume—were just horrific. The overbearing smell would leave you nauseated, wishing for subtle. Some fragrances work well together. These didn't. My friend Tina tells me this is always a tell-tale sign. The beginning stage. I should have known. It all makes sense.

I find a small black and white photo of my mom and dad, they're all dressed up, it appears they're at some type of affair. He in a suit, looking stunning, and she in a form-fitting, knee-length cocktail dress. Sexy. A pair of high-heel sling-backs, and opera-length pearls. And my guess is she is also wearing Chanel No. 5, a perfume she loved. She would dab it behind her ears, behind her knees, on her wrists and for good luck one more dab in her cleavage. And if by chance she was using cologne that had a spray nozzle, she would pump and spritz the bottle a couple of times into the air, and then walk through the mist.

She loved having just a hint of perfume or cologne on her skin.

I ask, on the off chance that this may spark a memory, if she remembers wearing Chanel perfume. She asks with great curiosity, "Chanel? Who's that?"

I go on this long-winded rant, telling her that Coco Chanel was a famous designer and she lived in Paris—Paris, France—and was sort of ahead of her time, but not really, because being ahead of your time really means that you are in fact an innovator, an original, someone who brings something new to the world, and I go on and on and on, and even I get completely confused and lost in my description. So I can just imagine that my mom hasn't a clue what I'm talking about. And then I just simply say "perfume," Chanel was a perfume that you really liked and wore all the time. And she smiles. A soft smile, which I interpret as some kind of remembrance. She closes her eyes and smiles, and I'm wondering—hoping—maybe she's remembering something lovely, like a date she had with my dad, or a dress she wore, or maybe the smell of the perfume.

And then she opens her eyes.

"I don't know," she says. "I can't."

She doesn't want to watch cartoons any longer. She wants to watch *Jesus* and asks me to change the channel to *the Jesus hour*. I don't really know what she's talking about, but I channel surf in the hopes that she will let out a whoop of sorts when I get to it.

It's a local evangelist who has his own TV show on a local cable station. A young man who my mom thinks is the cat's meow. She literally swoons as she watches him. He is young, he is vibrant, he is loud, and he is asking his congregation—both in the massive auditorium and at home—to pray to the almighty Jesus Christ to give them, each of them, strength and comfort, to give them a ray of hope in these dark, dreary financially unstable times, to put food on their plates and a hand to guide them, and as he closes his eyes and lifts his arms heaven bound, thank you, Jesus, thank you Jesus, our lord and savior, my mother, who is flat on her back on the recliner, lifts her arms and closes her eyes and sways back and forth and tells me how much she loves Jesus and I tell her that this man,

this evangelist, is not Jesus, and she says, "He's close enough."
And then she asks me if I love Jesus. I think about my friend
Patricia, and her advice, to just sort of go along with things,
keep it all simple, uncomplicated. So I say yes, I love Jesus.
And she asks, how much, and I say well, enough, and she asks
how much is enough, and I say, well, Mom, a good chunk. And
she says, "I love Jesus. I love him so much." And I say that's
wonderful, and she says yes, and then tells me that she wants
to go on the TV show and meet Jesus, and I tell her okay, and
she says let's go now, right now, and I say that you probably
need to get tickets to go on the TV show, or maybe, maybe
not tickets, but you can't just show up and she says I want to
go now. Right now. This minute. Take me now. I tell her that
I don't have a car, and she says that's okay, I have a car. It's a
brand-new car, that she just bought yesterday because she has
almost forty-three million dollars in the bank and she wants to
give it to Jesus, this Jesus on the TV, she wants to give him all
her money.

*"Sam," she screamed for my father while I was on the other end
of the phone, "she's becoming a goddamn Buddhist and I know,
I know she's going to give all these crazy people all of her money
and probably all her worldly possessions. I just know it." And
then back to me, "Are you joining the Moonies, or becoming one
of those orange people at the airport? Is this a cult?"*

It was 1975, I was nineteen years old, and I was living in
a studio apartment in New York City. I was working at a
clothing store in the West Village, a sort of hip, cool clothing
store right on West Eighth Street—right across from Electric
Ladyland, a recording studio, where tons of famous musicians

and their wives and/or groupies would come and go at all hours. It was then, at the age of nineteen, that I began practicing Buddhism. My folks never fostered or encouraged any kind of faith or religion; we were not practicing Jews, not by a long stretch. We were "Day Jews," a day here, a day there. I was searching for something, something that gave me a sense of self, a belief, and faith. A sense of belonging, and a sense of community. I found it through a girlfriend who began practicing Buddhism and encouraged me to come to an introductory meeting.

I told my mom that I had gone to a Buddhist meeting with Kyle, and that I loved it, and that I felt it was exactly what I needed and wanted, and just what I was looking for. In her typical fashion she asked me if I thought that maybe having a boyfriend might just quench the same thirst. I said no, this was not the same thing. She was absolutely, thoroughly convinced that I was going to hand my entire life, not to mention my small, "low two-figure" bank account, over to "these crazy, lunatic people." It was sort of one of those no, yes conversations—no, I wasn't, I told her; yes, you will, she said. *Mark my words, in a few months, you will be living on the streets, begging for food money, you will be barefoot and filthy and dirty, with matted, clumpy disgusting hair. And if I see you at Kennedy Airport with those fucking clackers in your fingers and you're wearing that fucking orange schmatte, do not say hello to me, because I will not know you."*

I took her to a Buddhist meeting with me. I wanted her to see with her own eyes, and hear with her own ears, what I had fallen in love with. The people, the chanting, the community.

I wanted to share this with her. She loved it. Every minute of it. When she drove me back to my apartment, she took my hand and her eyes filled up and she said, *"You found your joy. But please, promise me, if they start asking you to give them your money, or any of your clothing, I want you to tell them, very politely, to go fuck themselves." And then she said, "This is precisely why your father and I do not belong to a temple."*

I promised her.

"Promise me, Mom, promise me that you won't want to give him all your money."

"Why?"

"Well, for starters, you don't have forty-three million, and secondly, this guy, this guy is not Jesus. He's a Jesus wanna-be."

"Oh. Okay."

"Okay?"

"Yes. Okay. How much money do I have?"

"Not much."

"How much is not much?"

"Less than much."

"Okay."

THE SCREAMING STARTS UP AGAIN. This time it's nonstop. There is no inhaling and no exhaling. No breathing, there is no catching her breath. She opens her mouth and howls. Her whole face frozen in a scream. I try to comfort her and she pushes me away. A strong, forceful push. The kind of force I heard about from the two nurses' aides. My mother has a will and strength that aren't at all diminishing just because her mind is. She has amazing force and pushes me with her hand and I land right up against the wall. She is strong and defiant.

"No!"

I say Mom, please, *it's okay, it's okay, it's okay.*

No, she says, it's not okay. It. Is. Not. Okay.

She hates that I see her like this. I can tell by how she is looking at me. She hates that I see her like this. Even though at that moment I don't think she even recognizes me.

One nurse comes rushing in and along, with her, the neighbor who wants to know who is being killed, where is the murder? I tell her that no one is being killed. No one. She calls me a liar and wants me arrested. "Pants on fire," she says. I tell the nurse to please, please, please take this woman back to her room. My mother continues screaming, a continual guttural sound. Then the woman, the neighbor, begins to sing an aria, or at least it sounds very much operatic. And really quite good. *Aha! I get it, it all becomes clear to me, this woman must have been an opera singer and my mother being my mother has to compete with her.* So, she tells everyone that she is a very famous opera singer, which will fulfill my mom's personal intent—to put a sharp pin in someone else's balloon. On the count of three, we lift my mom and put her in the wheelchair, and her neighbor just stands there watching this, and I can feel my mom's embarrassment and humiliation. I take my mom, and I comfort her, massaging her back, stroking her hair, she seems to calm down, catch her breath, she tells me I'm pretty, "Oh, you're so pretty, beautiful, just beautiful," she doesn't know who I am. She doesn't know that I'm her daughter. I grab her hand and I don't know why I say this, maybe I think it will make her feel better or feel special, particularly in front of her nosy neighbor, and of course I now feel completely conspiratorial, but I ask my mom if she wants to go see Jesus. Jesus, she says, really, oh, yes, yes, yes, I want to see Jesus. Yes. Thank you. You're so pretty, thank you. The neighbor chimes in, and she says that she wants to go see Jesus, too. I tell her that no, not this time, this time she can't come with us and see Jesus. Then my mother says to the neighbor, "Oh, sure, now you want to see Jesus, go fuck yourself, you bitch." The neighbor calls her a smelly fish, my mother retaliates by calling her a smelly fish fuck-face, and then I ask the nurse if maybe we can prevent this from continuing any further by please, please, taking this neighbor back to her room so we can all have a moment or two of calm.

Never in my life have I wanted calm more. And I am not a seeker of calm. Ken is. Ken loves calm and mellow and comfort and ease. Although he has moments—big huge moments—of being chaotic, completely chaotic, like when we have to be at the airport to catch a flight, he does everything, including packing, at the very last minute. This does not include the "Where are the passports, and shit, holy shit, I can't find my wallet" nut dance. This is a whole separate dance routine. The losing-of-the-wallet waltz. Included in this is a full chorus line. This drives me nuts. Completely and utterly nuts. He's had an entire week to get his shit together and now at nine-thirty in the morning he's washing his fucking clothing and has no idea where his wallet is. *Excuse me, Ken, we have a one o'clock flight. Excuse me, Amy, but I can't find the passports or my wallet. You know what, Ken, what was wrong with last night? You had an entire night to pack and look for this stuff. I had the wallet this morning, Amy, and now I can't find it. You know what, Ken, do me a favor, do me a fucking favor, go to Paris all by yourself, and when you get there, send me a postcard wishing, hoping, begging I was with you at the Louvre.*

Other than airport-travel frenzy craziness, Ken is generally very calm, and at ease. This whole situation would throw him into a tailspin.

And at that very moment, my cell phone rings, and it is Ken and my mother is screaming in the background, and he asks me what's going on, what's that noise, and I walk out to the hallway, so I can hear him, and he can hear me, and I tell him that it is my mom screaming, that she screams and it's a part of the disease and she's afraid, and he says, "But it doesn't sound human." I tell him I'll call him back.

"Bitch." The neighbor calls her.

"Shit heel." My mother points to the door. "I don't like your face. Leave."

The nurse informs me that they actually like each other, and the cursing and emotion go hand and hand. A small piece of the whole puzzle. And then my mom asks me, as if out of nowhere, how many babies do I have. I tell her none. She says, Oh, no, you have a baby. I say no, she says yes . . . no, yes, and then I say, "No, Mom, I had an abortion."

No, yes . . . no, yes.

I know *intuitively* this isn't going to work. She can't remember, she thinks she had six babies, and one with Jesus. She is not going to remember that I in fact do not have children and had an abortion (a few, to be more exact). She imagines, or maybe she even believes, that she has had many babies. She has mistaken my niece and nephew as her children. She doesn't see them as her grandchildren. She has also told everyone that she had a baby, a gorgeous baby boy, and one day when they were in the park, many, many, many years ago, the baby boy was snatched away, taken from her, and kidnapped, and she tells this to anyone and everyone. From the waitstaff to the hairdresser to a stranger in the elevator, and of course because it's such a sad and horrific tale, this garners great attention. And the more attention it gains, the more fabricated it becomes, embellished as time goes by. At one point the baby boy had been found, and he was working in the circus, or on the train or at Applebee's, where he was a waiter. Oh, yes, she says, the police found him, and then when she sees that the happy ending isn't going to create more sympathy for her, she goes straight down another road. "But then he was murdered at Applebee's."

Square one.

"An abortion? You had an abortion," the neighbor says with a tone that is both curious and repulsive. "Aren't you Jewish?" "No," my mother says in a defiant tone, "she's not Jewish," and then my mom turns to me, "What are you?" she asks. "I'm a Buddhist," I say. My mom repeats that—she's a Buddhist—and then she says to her neighbor, "Time to leave, Ethel; you've worn out your welcome."

The neighbor (whose real name is not Ethel, it's just what my mom calls her) and the nurse leave. I pull a chair right next to the recliner and hold my mom's hand. I throw a blanket on top of her. It's her new favorite blanket. I am exhausted. This is exhausting.

"An abortion?" She asks. "What's that?"

"It's when you don't want the baby."

"I didn't either," she says.

"You wanted an abortion?" I ask.

"Oh, yes."

"What happened?"

"I had you."

I'm not sure if she is talking about me, or a make-believe pregnancy, or if this is her talking or the dementia talking. It's so hard to tell where it all ends and begins. But there is a ten-year difference between my brother and me. And I wonder if she tried getting pregnant or didn't want to get pregnant, or maybe in those ten years she lost a baby, or miscarried, and there is a god-awful feeling, a sad, overwhelming feeling right there right smack center in my belly, a feeling that perhaps fifty-four years earlier I in fact was not wanted, or wished for, or hoped for. I was a decision she made. Or maybe a decision not made, or maybe it was made for her. Or maybe they flipped a coin, and clearly my dad won. There is just something that cuts straight through you when you hear that you were not wanted and there was a chance that had she gone along with her own decision, the one she wanted, I would not be here. At all. My friend Amy would tell me it was because I was so determined to be in the world that nothing my mom could or would have done would have prevented that from occurring. I would like to believe—even subconsciously, and viscerally—that much was at work that played right straight into my favor that day. It's all so confusing.

AND PAINFUL.

I was twenty-two.

I got pregnant. I told my folks.

I had already had one abortion when I was seventeen years old. That first time I was all alone, and I sat there in the clinic, in the waiting room with five other young women, who were probably no older than I was, who were waiting for the doctor so they, too, could terminate their unwanted pregnancies. I felt such profound shame and guilt. I was alone, and the emptiness and the sorrow I felt before and after—the terminating of one life, and not knowing or understanding enough about my own, not knowing who I was in the world. My own worth. I didn't want to have a baby; it would be a horrific mistake. All these girls, young women sitting there, one reading a magazine, one lost in thought, one doing her homework, one with a friend with her, another with her boyfriend, who was holding her hand, comforting her. I realized in that moment, it wasn't just about having an abortion, it was about not having enough self-worth to prevent this from happening—*and I was alone.* Sitting there, all alone. And I would leave alone, and I would leave much emptier than when I came in.

Then later I told my parents I was pregnant and that I was going to have an abortion, and at that time in my life, I was not alone, I had friends, really good friends, and my father and my mother took unbelievable care of me. My father made sure that I had the best doctor, and I was not going to be in a clinic, I was admitted into Flower Fifth Hospital, which is now Beth Israel Hospital, and had my abortion and stayed the night, and when all was said and done, my mother stayed by my side, right there curled up on the hospital bed next to me, and she didn't leave me, not for one minute.

Maybe, maybe she saw herself in me.

She needs to get some sleep.

It is time for me to go back to the hotel.

It is late. We're both tired.

They have given her some pills, and she is dozing. I kiss her good night, she takes my hand, kisses my fingers, and she says,

"Good night, my *letter.*"

"Good night, my envelope."

I am in great need of both fresh air and Ken.

And a glass of wine.

NOT NECESSARILY IN THAT ORDER.

I draw a bath. I pour myself a glass of wine, because I decide it's best to buy a bottle at the liquor store, which is much cheaper than buying by the glass, particularly when staying at a hotel, and besides, I know I'm not stopping at one glass. It is quiet. I soak, and I sip, and I add some bubbles, and I roll up a towel and I place it behind my head, resting on my neck, so when I lean back on the rim of the tub, my neck doesn't hurt. I want comfort. I close my eyes, and all I can see is my mom on her recliner, shriveled up, and I feel scared and sad, and I hope, I really, truly deeply out-loud hope, that if it ever comes to this, if I end up like this, shriveled up with no memory and only an occasional flash of someone or something, I want someone, preferably someone who really likes me, to put me out of my misery. And I want it done fast. I do believe that one should die with dignity. And it should be their choice of how they would like to die. And if I am given the opportunity to choose how I would like to die, if there happens to be a reality show, called *The Hereafter,* and I get chosen to be on that show, to be a contestant, where one can chose their own mode of death, this is how I would choose to die: in my husband's arms, surrounded by my friends, and Whitney Houston, pre–Bobby Brown, will be standing at the foot of the bed, singing her version of "And I Will Always Love You." Ken of course would add "great sex" to the mix, but since it is my choice how I would like to spend my last evening on earth, I only want him, friends, and Whitney, and perhaps, if there is time, maybe watch a great movie. And he and I would be fighting about this to my death. I know this for a fact, I know the last words I would hear before I closed my eyes to the world would be, "But I just took a Cialis." And if by chance I didn't die that night, he would have a good thirty-six hours to try to convince me.

I add more hot water to the tub, and I begin to think about the fact that my brother lives twenty minutes away and that we don't speak, or communicate, and here I am in a hotel in Albuquerque, New Mexico, and I am all alone, and how profoundly sad that is. And then I realize how sad it must be for him to know that his only sister is twenty minutes away and that he doesn't pick up the phone to ask, *"How are you, how is Mom, how was Mom when she saw you, did she know who you were, does she recognize you, was it sad, or strange, would you like to come over and have dinner, or drinks?"* or just: *"How about coming by and visiting with us, just to say hello."*

I am emotional. It just pours out of me.

Thinking about my mom, death, the hereafter, the day after, the morning after, my sweet husband, my gorgeous friends, and my father, I think about my dad, who would be appalled, absolutely appalled, that my mother is spending much too much time on the recliner.

I call Ken and cry. He comforts me.
I call Amy and cry. She comforts me.
I call Peter and we commiserate.
I call Marcia and she makes me laugh.
I call Tina and Patricia and leave them both messages since neither is home.

Then I turn on the TV, the news. Breaking news. Breaking news is never good. There's been a plane crash in New York City, a plane has gone down, and it has landed in the Hudson River, apparently some birds—geese, a flock of geese—flew straight into the engine, and caused the engines to stop, and the plane went down, but it appears that all the passengers and crew members on the flight have survived, and the pilot, someone named Sully, is extraordinary, amazing, a saint, and it's a miracle, a miracle plane crash, and the plane is in the Hudson River and . . .

. . . I am flying home tomorrow.

This is the second plane crash that I have heard about or read about in two weeks. The first was fatal. No survivors.

"It comes in threes, always in threes. Death, accidents, and bad news. Threes." My mother always reminded me of this

when someone died, or when there was an accident, or a plane crash. If there was a famous person who died, two others would die that week, if there was a car crash, or car wreck, two others would happen within a five-mile radius within the next few weeks, and if there was a plane crash, then of course, there would be two more. There had to be. This was a rule.

A law.

Unbreakable.

I take an Ambien, I shut the lights, and I lie there. In the dark. I can't sleep. I just can't sleep. So much is swirling around. Pieces of a life. My life, her life. Our life. Wishing I could turn back the clock, change or reverse some moments, redo some years, love her more, wishing she could have loved me better. But I know that everything that happens—everything—brings you to where it is you need to be, where you are, I know this. I know that my life, every crease, every flaw, every seemingly bad or awful or horrible mistake I have made, got me to the next place that I needed to be and therefore it is not really a mistake. Every fuck-up, every bad move, every pain and suffering, got me to here. Right here. This place. This hotel, at this moment, wide awake. And I regret none of it. Not one bit of it. Okay, maybe one or two bits. But I can see in her eyes in her face in her creases in her body that she has too many regrets and pains and wishes—to rewind, and to re-create. There is so much that she can't take back and change. She kept it inside, buried, she always, always called herself an ostrich, her head always in the sand, she hated to hear bad news, bad news was not allowed. She hated to hear sad news, or problems, or pain. Oh, god, she hated pain. Anyone and everyone's pain. Physical, mental, emotional, any kind of pain. It was too messy for her. And it was a conflict—she was conflicted—because how can you bear to see your children or grandchildren or husband in pain and not wish that somehow it could be removed or taken away. But there were moments, big gigantic huge "mom/mother/mommy" moments when she rose to the occasion—really, truly, profoundly rose to the occasion—and I am sure, she shocked even herself.

She kept all her sorrow and shame and guilt and pain inside. Buried. Deep. Inside. She mistook sharing and giving and being open about her feelings for weakness, and being cared for, which is different from being taken care of, with pity. She had no clue that by burying it, keeping it hidden, one day it would all show up again. She didn't know that she would one day be wearing—on her face, in her eyes—all that she kept buried.

"I will never be a burden," she said. "Never!" This right after my father died. "I will never be a burden and I need no one to take care of me. I can take care of myself, and I'm telling you right now, I will never become like those other old needy biddies, who depend on their children and their friends and that will never be me. That I can promise. I will never be a burden."

She never—not once—talked about it, or mentioned it, or spoke its name. She never talked about her pain or suffering or uneasiness or fear or unhappiness or feelings or, god forbid, hormonal imbalance. She didn't know what it was that was making her so unhappy, so fragile, so restless, so jittery, so angry, so sad, so moody. She didn't know that it had a name, and every single woman on our street, on our block, in our neighborhood, was probably going through something just as similar, as scary, as unsettling. An epidemic of sorts. The crazy neighbor who threw all her husband's clothing out of the window while he was at work, the other neighbor who lived across the street and then one day, all of a sudden, had to *go away* for a month, and then there was the neighbor—a family acquaintance—who made her husband and two children breakfast, kissed them goodbye, got into her brand-new hot-off-the-conveyor-belt Chevrolet Caprice, which was parked in the locked two-car garage, laid down on the back seat until the carbon monoxide took her life. Her husband found her. And no one talked about this. No one. There were warning signs—depression, sadness, forgetfulness, emptiness, wanting to be alone, pills and liquor, crying, anger, mood swings.

My mother would sit on the edge of the bed, wearing only panties and a bra, and she would chain smoke, one cigarette after another, and she would just sit there, on the edge on the bed, watching TV, and she would cry. And cry. And cry. Every. Single. Morning. And she would leave the bedroom door ajar, and when I would pass her room, I would see her sitting, crying, cigarette in one hand, remote in the other. And my favorite days, my very all-time favorite days, the ones that I loved the most, were the days when I got to stay home from school because of snow days, or sick days, or just because she said I could stay home, those were my favorite days, because I would sit right next to her, on the edge of the bed, with my legs dangling, and I would tell her, "It's okay, Mommy, it's okay."

I am eleven years old.

I have the measles.

The doctor tells my mother it is the worst case of measles she (yes, I had a female pediatrician) has ever seen. Some kid in school had the measles, and it was contagious, and I got it. It started out on my head, and then it spread to every single part of my body—I had measles everywhere: in my vagina, in my ears, on my head, on my face, and in my throat. I am itching all over. I am in excruciating pain when I pee. It burns. My mom is told that I need to be sponged down with a cool compress every few hours, to apply ointments over the rash, and I am to take oral medication, along with being kept hydrated. I have a raging fever of 104. I don't remember if there was a shot involved. There might have been. The doctor tells her that (a) I am very, very contagious, and that (b) I need to be isolated for at least four days. My mother informs my father that he needs to stay in my bedroom, or the guest room, which was once my brother's room but since he no longer lives at home, it is now the guest room–slash–TV room, that I am going to stay in their bedroom with her and she is going to take care of me and stay with me. The fever spikes, the cool compresses aren't helping, and she makes me chicken noodle soup (*okay,* Campbell's Chicken Noodle Soup) and my very favorite sandwiches—peanut butter and jelly on white bread, and tuna salad on toasted rye. And pickles, I love pickles. She crawls into bed with me and we watch television and she keeps me cool with the compresses and she is worried and she calls my Aunt Gertie, who tells her to give me a baby aspirin, even though the doctor didn't prescribe it because sometimes a baby aspirin can bring down the fever. The fever starts to break, the compresses begin to cool me down, and the ointment starts to work—the itching slowly but surely begins to ease. She doesn't go bowling, she doesn't see her friends, she doesn't go to a dinner party that she and my father were invited to, she doesn't go to Brooklyn to visit with her sisters or her brother or even to see her mother and father, my grandparents. She stays with me.

We are watching *The Carol Burnett Show,* she is on her side of the bed, I am on my dad's side, and one of the guests is pregnant and my mother decides right then and there that it is a good time to tell me all about the birds and the bees.

A man is a farmer, she says, and the woman is a field, and sometimes the man goes out to the field and he decides he wants to start a garden. So he lies down on the field and he rolls around, and he laughs and he plays and then he starts planting some seeds, and the next thing you know, nine months later, a flower blooms and then from that flower, a baby is born.

I tell her that's not how a baby is born. That I already learned in school, during hygiene class, when they showed us the movie all about how to use Kotex sanitary napkins, and the sanitary napkin belt, and the whole story about menstruation. I tell her that a man and a woman have sex, that he puts his penis in her vagina and then there's the whole sperm and egg thing, the sperm attaching itself to the egg, and then the woman gets pregnant and a baby is born.

And to think, I end up marrying a gardener.

I get up to pee.

It is the middle of the night.
And as I pass the mirrored closet, I catch myself—my reflection—in the full-length mirror.

This is what I see:

A body that is no longer thin or sleek, straight or narrow.
A body that is fragile, small, and so very tired.

Short, wavy thick hair streaked with much gray.
Thin, straight hair that is now completely gray.

Hands that hurt upon waking and are arthritic in the winter months.
Hands that hurt upon waking and are arthritic and curled all year long.

Knees that can no longer bend easily when I pray.
Knees that can no longer bend.

A stomach that is a bit more round.
A stomach that has shrunken completely.

A waist that is no longer twenty-four inches.
A waist that has disappeared.

A face filled with small lines, some of which are from laughter and great joy, and some from sorrow and sadness.
A face filled with deep lines, some of which are from unhappiness, fear, and deep regret, and others from great joy,

and laughter.

Eyes that twinkle—really, deeply twinkle; dance out-loud twinkle.
Eyes that no longer twinkle, that are often empty and blank.

A mouth that laughs heartily, that screams loudly, that curses boldly, that can rip through your gut or melt your heart.
A mouth that no longer can form sentences, or speak words, and wants to. Really truly wants to.

AND I CAN SEE MY HEART. AND I CAN SEE HER HEART.

And truthfully, honestly, it is really one and the same, the same exact heart. Filled with memories, many, many memories. My gorgeous, imperfect, lived-to-the-fullest life. Her gorgeous, imperfect, lived-to-the-fullest life.

And as I look at my reflection in the mirror, as I stand there naked, I see a strong, independent, creative, emotional, by-the-seat-of-your-pants, impulsive, joyous, funny, willful, powerful, strident, passionate, talented, happily married, *and childless* woman. And I realize, I deeply profoundly realize and know in that moment that I am in fact—that I have become—the woman, the very woman, whom my mother had always wanted and wished to be.

She is on her recliner.
It is early morning.
She is being fed some breakfast. "Ca-ca," she says and spits it out.

I am there for a few hours before I take off and return home. The nurse tells me that she had a good night, that she slept, and that she didn't seem to be restless. Sometimes she's just so restless, she tries to crawl out of bed, and then they have to mount some pillow bolsters on either side of her so she doesn't fall out of the bed.

She looks at me.

Curious.

SHE CAN'T PLACE ME.

But she stares. She stares and stares, and then she says she wants to watch television. I channel surf: the Cartoon Network, she shakes her head no, no cartoons; the news, she shakes her head no, no news; an old black and white movie, she shakes her head no, no old movies; and I am channel surfing, and all of a sudden, in a perfect full screen close-up, is George Clooney, and the movie is *Ocean's Eleven*, and it is on cable, and my mom is swooning. Swooning. She cannot contain herself.

I am sitting next to her in a chair, and she nudges me, and then she pinches my arm, and she says with sheer confidence, with a thrill in her voice, as if it were really truly deeply possible:

"I would fuck him."

"I would marry him," I say with equal enthusiasm. "I would

marry George Clooney."

And without missing a beat, she says:

"*Oh, Amy, you've always been such a dreamer.*"

Sweet dreams, mom.

ACKNOWLEDGMENTS

THANK YOU SO . . .

Frances Gould-Naftal
Robyn Hatcher
Patricia Elam
Jeffrey Seeds
Carla Singer
Barbara DeVries Gordon
Josephine (Josie) Schoel
Shari Levine
Marcia G. Yerman

for reading, rereading, rereading, loving me, loving this book.

Peter Werner, for being the very best guy friend a girl can have.
Amy Parker Litzenberger, for being the best girl friend a girl
can have, and for being a true soul mate.

KEN, FOR LOVING ME LIKE CRAZY—I AM SO VERY
DELIGHTED THAT YOU ARE MY HUSBAND.

CAROL KIMMELMAN-GOULD,
for being the woman I always wanted to be when I grew up.

Because . . .

I have a ton of women friends. Really. Friends are vital. Profoundly. They truly keep us going. I am fortunate beyond words to always have a great many women friends in my life. I treasure them with all my heart.

In no particular order, I would like to acknowledge them:

Terri Johnson

Maryanne Ruby

Carolyn Howard Johnson

Michael Trenner

Karen Kontizas

Tina Smith

Claire O. Moed

Marianne Moloney

Holly Stein

Kedren Werner

Roberta Friedman

Beth Fraikorn

Rozanna Weinberger

Jeri Love

Maleyne Syracuse

Martha Lorin

Donna Hamilton

Juli Leventen

Caroline Case

Jean Work

Nancy Isola

Julie Ann Larsen

ABOUT THE
AUTHOR

© KEN FERRIS

AMY FERRIS is an author, a screenwriter, and an editor.
She is on the advisory board of the Women's Media
Center, the Executive Board of Directors at Peter's Valley
Arts, Education & Craft Center, and the Advisory Board
of the Women's Educational Center. She is a passionate
champion for any and all things women related. She lives in
Pennsylvania with her delightful husband Ken and . . . yes,
she is wide awake at 3:00 AM.

Selected Titles from Seal Press

For more than thirty years, Seal Press has published groundbreaking books. By women. For women. Visit our website at www.sealpress.com. Check out the Seal Press blog at www.sealpress.com/blog.

RESCUE ME, HE'S WEARING A MOOSE HAT: AND 40 OTHER DATES AFTER 50, by Sherry Halperin. $13.95, 1-58005-068-9. The hilarious account of a woman who finds herself back in the dating scene after midlife.

TANGO: AN ARGENTINE LOVE STORY, by Camille Cusumano. $15.95, 1-58005-250-9. The spicy travel memoir of a woman who left behind a failed fifteen-year relationship and fell in love with Argentina through the dance that embodies intensity, freedom, and passion.

FOR KEEPS: WOMEN TELL THE TRUTH ABOUT THEIR BODIES, GROWING OLDER, AND ACCEPTANCE, edited by Victoria Zackheim. $15.95, 1-58005-204-5. This inspirational collection of personal essays explores the relationship that aging women have with their bodies.

SWEET CHARLOTTE'S SEVENTH MISTAKE, by Cori Crooks. $18.95, 1-58005-249-5. In this stunning visual memoir, Cori Crooks searches for her identity among the old photographs, diary entries, and letters left behind by her delinquent family.

BETTER THAN I EVER EXPECTED: STRAIGHT TALK ABOUT SEX AFTER SIXTY, by Joan Price. $15.95, 1-58005-152-9. A warm, witty, and honest book that contends with the challenges and celebrates the delights of older-life sexuality.

P.S.: WHAT I DIDN'T SAY, edited by Megan McMorris. $15.95, 1-58005-290-8. For the friend who's been there for you through everything, the friend you've lost touch with, or the friend you've wished you could help, this thought-provoking collection of unsent letters expresses the unspoken.